Live Issues:

Reflections on the
Human Condition

Live Issues:

Reflections on the
Human Condition

Mavis Klein

**PSYCHE
BOOKS**

Winchester, UK
Washington, USA

First published by Psyche Books, 2013
Psyche Books is an imprint of John Hunt Publishing Ltd., Laurel House, Station Approach,
Alresford, Hants, SO24 9JH, UK
office1@jhpbooks.net
www.psyche-books.com

For distributor details and how to order please visit the 'Ordering' section on our website.

Text copyright: Mavis Klein 2012

ISBN: 978 1 78099 828 2

A CIP catalogue record for this book is available from the British Library.

Design: Stuart Davies

Printed and bound by CPI Group (UK) Ltd, Croydon, CR0 4YY

We operate a distinctive and ethical publishing philosophy in all
areas of our business, from our global network of authors to
production and worldwide distribution.

CONTENTS

For Maia, Leila, Helena, and Benjamin – and to life

Preface

This book is informed by my love of philosophical, psychological and spiritual theories of the human condition, and my desire to share with a wide public those theories I have tried and tested over many years and which continue to delight me.

My first two loves were the apparently irreconcilable and mutually hostile psychological theories of Freud and the behaviourist B. F. Skinner. True believers in the former dismiss the latter as dangerous, mechanistic, simplistic, dehumanising, trivial nonsense, while the committed experimentalists of the latter school go to considerable lengths to prove the former pernicious, unscientific, tautological, mythological rubbish.

But they found their perfect reconciliation for me in my third love, Transactional Analysis. Psychoanalysis stops when revelation is considered complete. Purely behavioural therapies discount the necessity of revelation. Transactional Analysis was the first of the now many psychological theories and therapies that pursue meaning and adaptive behavioural change hand-in-hand. Transactional Analysis has been my lingua franca as a psychotherapist for the past thirty-five years.

But when I had already been a practising psychotherapist for a number of years my mind and spirit were blown wide open by the evidence of astrology. Once again, I believed I was faced with an irreconcilable conflict; I must either declare my allegiance to Freud's position that we are all born tabula rasa, on which our personalities and characters are etched by the earliest experiences of our lives; *or* I must disavow the primacy of 'nurture' in bowing to the deterministic primacy of 'nature' implicit in astrology.

It took me a number of years of struggling through the highways and byways of fate and free-will, contingency and determinism to realise that these dualities were two sides of one coin. I hope the essays in this book will bear witness to my achieved reconciliation of 'nature' and 'nurture' in my presumption of the validity of both humanistic psychology *and* astrology, which I now use in parallel rather than in combat in everyday life.

Most serious books are thought marathons; this serious book is a collection of thought sprints. I hope they set your pulse racing.

Introduction

Transactional Analysis (or TA as it is familiarly called) is the creation of the Canadian-born psychiatrist Eric Berne (1910-70).

In 1956, after more than a decade of being in a training analysis, the San Francisco Psychoanalytic Institute rejected Berne's application for certification as a psychoanalyst, deeming him 'not ready'. This failure intensified his long-standing ambition to add something new to psychoanalysis, and he was now determined to 'show them' with a completely new approach to psychotherapy.

The essential disagreement between Berne and establishment psychoanalysis concerned practice, not theory. He was, and remained all his life, committed to orthodox psychoanalytic theory, but his frustration with the slowness of psychoanalysis, as therapy, to effect measurable change in his patients made him baulk at the overly passive role demanded of the analyst. He questioned the assumptions behind the procedures of psychoanalysis as therapy, and he decided that in one respect they were false. Where psychoanalysis insisted that unconscious conflicts must be resolved before manifest personality changes could be effectively and permanently achieved, Berne claimed that patients could be made better *first* – and quickly – and have their underlying conflicts resolved later (if required). Thus, out of a practical concern to cure people quickly, TA came into being, and developed as a theoretical elaboration of psychoanalytic ego psychology and a systematised approach to ego therapy.

What distinguishes TA from other theoretical elaborations of the ego is that its concepts are direct derivatives of psychoanalysis as a whole. The Parent, Adult and Child ego states are exact derivatives of the superego, ego, and id, but describe the here-and-nowness of our conscious lives. What Berne proposed was essentially Freud without the unconscious. Berne realised that the core existential reality of any human being is accessible through the conscious and pre-conscious ego, and can be revealed by a skilled psychotherapist in a few hours rather than a few years!

This is so, argued Berne, because the experiences we have in the later stages of our childhood development are, through the influence of the 'repetition compulsion', very similar to the primary experiences of the first six years of our lives. And, unlike the repressed experiences of our earliest years (which can take years to tease into consciousness) our most significant experiences after the age of six are available to our pre-conscious minds and can quickly be brought into full consciousness.

TA speaks the deep truths that psychoanalysis and the greatest writers have always known, and it speaks these truths with enormous clarity, precision and concision and without any loss of meaning. As theory, it makes sane the previous schizoid fragmentation of psychology into theories that were either precise and meaningless or profoundly true but inoperative.

The concept of the ego states and the delineation of their natures is undoubtedly the central genius of TA theory and therapy. But what makes TA more than 'psychoanalysis without the unconscious' is its concepts of strokes, for which TA is indebted to 'operant conditioning', the learning theory of the behaviourist psychologist, B. F. Skinner. Thus TA is a highly successful marriage of the most unlikely bedfellows, psychoanalysis and behaviourism. It is both 'hard' and 'soft', diagnostic and prescriptive, subjective and objective, holistic and atomistic, and its basic concepts are so easily understood that they can be communicated with ease to even very young children.

Eric Berne wrote six books on TA, beginning with *Transactional Analysis in Psychotherapy*, first published in 1961, and culminating in *What Do You Say After You Say Hello?* published posthumously in 1970. *Games People Play*, published in 1964, became a worldwide bestseller, and the concept of 'playing games' has permeated everyday language, and is at least vaguely under-stood and referred to by people who have never even heard of Transactional Analysis.

Since January 1971, the official organ of the International Transactional Analysis Association (headquarters in San Francisco) has been the quarterly *Transactional Analysis Journal*, in whose pages TA theory and application have continued to evolve. Many important concepts now familiarly used by TA therapists and teachers were only incipient in *What Do You Say After You Say Hello?* but fortunately there have been many brilliant followers of Berne, in whose minds these ideas have germinated and been brought to life. (The elaboration of the development of the ego states in childhood, explications of ego state contaminations and exclusions, and my theory of 'five personality types' are my own contributions to evolving TA theory, all of which are elaborated in my book, *Pain and Joy in Intimate Relationships*.)

TA has now achieved the status of being a consistent and comprehensive psychological theory of child development, individual differences, pathology and therapy.

As well as being a very popular form of humanistic 'cognitive behavioural therapy', TA is now widely taught in educational and business settings throughout the world. The British Institute of Transactional Analysis was the first TA organisation to be formed outside the United States, in 1974, followed by the formation of the European Association for Transactional Analysis (EATA), in 1975. Both are still flourishing.

Ego States

Over the past forty years I have been greatly facilitated in all my thinking by the wonderful language of Transactional Analysis.

In the interests of ease and concision of expression for both myself and the reader I ask leave occasionally to interpolate a little of the basic vocabulary of TA into the essays that follow. On most of the occasions when I do so, the meaning will be self-evident from the context, but for those readers who feel the need for illuminating elaboration, reference to this essay, the following one and the Glossary at the end of this book will be useful.

The basic interest of TA is the study of ego states. Ego states are not roles, but real, separate parts of each of us which together make up our sense of self. We are always *in* one or other of our ego states. Existentially, throughout our waking lives, we move around among these states of being, hour by hour, minute by minute, second by second. Our three principal ego states are called our Parent, our Adult and our Child. They began their formulation in Eric Berne's mind in 1957, consequent on the now legendary anecdote about the New York lawyer who, in response to Berne's question, 'How are you?' answered, 'Are you talking to the big-shot lawyer or the little boy, Doc?'

The concept of the ego states explicitly accounts for the reality that our conscious egos are divided into discrete selves that may or may not agree with each other on any given issue in life. Awareness of the separateness of our ego states gains us permission to experience ourselves as necessarily inconsistent – a simple truth that I have seen provide immense relief for many self-anguished people.

Our ego states have *structure*, that is their ideational content, which varies from one human being to another; and they have their universal energetic *functions*. (Implicit in TA theory, as in psychoanalysis, is the assumption that the mind is a reservoir of a fixed amount of psychic energy, which energy can be invested or withdrawn from ideas, objects and various functions of the living organism. The total amount of psychic energy in individuals varies, but for each individual the amount is constant.)

The Child ego state contains our *feelings*. Its function is to express itself. At birth we have only our Child, and only that part of the Child called *the Natural Child*. All our energy is contained in it. Its structure is simple; it is miserable or content; and functionally it expresses itself in a demanding, self-centred, lovable, spontaneous, totally uninhibited way. By about halfway through the first year of life, some energy is released from the Natural Child to form a new component of the whole Child ego state, called *the Little Professor*, which represents the infant's dawning awareness of the separateness of itself from the rest of the universe. It is manifest in the crawling, exploring, and 'getting into things'; it is the beginning of intuition and will, later in life, be a component of all creative thinking. It is still part of the Child, but is the precursor of the true (thinking) Adult ego state. The development and expression of the Natural Child and the Little Professor is hard-wired into our biology and, together, they are designated *the Free Child*. The third (and final) component of the Child is *the Adapted Child*, which begins its development towards the end of the first year of life when, in the interests of self-preservation and socialisation, it is necessary for caretakers to impose *inhibitions on the Free Child*. The structure of any individual's Adapted Child is determined by the particular 'Don'ts' imposed on the child at this stage. The Adapted Child is, by definition, in conflict with the unbridled impulses of the Natural Child and the Little Professor. It is the precursor of *the Parent ego state*.

The Adult ego state is our storehouse of facts and skills gained from the environment. Its function is to process and store infor-mation. It is our Adult that asks Why and What and When and

How and Where and Who. And it is with our Adult that we learn how to blow our noses, build a tower of blocks, use the toilet, wash and dry our hands, draw a picture, dress ourselves and tie our shoelaces. It is our Adult that knows the trick of peeling onions without crying, that can touch type, that budgets our income and expenditure, knows enough French to get by on a holiday in France, reads manuals and recipes and instructions for filling in a form.

Our Adult is without feeling. It expresses itself as objective thinking. It begins its development at about one year of age and has its most rapid development between the ages of about one-and-a-half and three, when it is particularly associated with the child learning to talk; and it has another period of rapid development in latency (about six to twelve years of age).

The Parent ego state contains our taught concepts of life, the values and generalisations given to us by our parents and other influential people in our lives. Its function is to nurture and control ourselves and others in accordance with our own principles and values.

As well as reflecting what each of our parents taught us, our Parent also reflects values that operate in society as a whole. In fact, there are probably a few Parent values that are common to all societies, such as that murder is wrong, as is sex between parents and their children or between brothers and sisters. In our particular society, kindness, tolerance, achievement, honesty, truthfulness, reliability, generosity and good manners are examples of positive Parent values that most people are taught; and violence, brutality, meanness, dishonesty, laziness, and bad manners are considered by most people to be negative Parent traits.

Each family, as well as having values that are shared by most people in the society of which the family is a part, usually have particular values of their own, often handed down from generation to generation. Some families, for example, are very keen on educational attainment, some value financial success, some value being of service to the community. Some families are religious, some intellectual, and some place great value on family life.

When we are in our Parent we are usually behaving like one of our parents did or in accordance with precepts they taught us when young, although our Parent is capable of change and growth throughout our lives. We may reject old values and acquire new ones as a consequence of new experiences and meetings with admired people. Our Parent ego state is essentially formed in the Oedipal stage of development (three to six years of age), from which we emerge *emotionally literate* (or not) in accordance with the precepts we are explicitly *taught* at that stage. (While we seem to be pre-programmed to be especially receptive to moral instruction at this stage of life, without explicit instruction our Parent remains essentially empty; the psychopathic personality is the extreme outcome.)

Other species have Child ego states, including the Adapted Child (especially evident in domesticated animals) and, it is inferred, some Adult; but only human beings have a Parent. Parental behaviour in other species is informed essentially by hard-wired Free Child instinct (although animals brought up in isolation are usually singularly inept in parenting their own offspring, which suggests that the Adapted Child also plays a part in other species' parenting of their young). But only human beings sit around in their Parent ego states arguing about right and wrong, life and death, philosophy, science, art, literature ...

People vary in the relative dominance of each ego state in their total makeup, which accounts for human variety.

Parent-type people tend to put their moral principles above all else, and look at life in terms of 'right versus wrong' and 'good versus bad'. They are honest, kind, reliable, solid citizens. Other people tend to respond to them with compliance and respect or angry rebelliousness.

Adult-type people tend to value most highly their own and

other people's rationality. They are clear-headed, practical and knowledgeable. Other people tend to seek them out for some specific purpose, such as their professional knowledge.

Child-type people are basically emotional and respond to life impulsively. They tend to be excitable, charming and fun-loving, but quite inconsiderate of other people's wishes and needs.

A completely balanced person has his energy evenly distributed between his three ego states, but such a perfect balance is rare. And it would be a pretty dull world if we were all so balanced. We need people with a little extra Parent to be our good doctors and nurses and counsellors and ministers of religion. We need people with a little extra Adult to be our good lawyers and scientists and research workers and computer operators. And we need people with a little extra Child to be our good artists and entertainers and inventors and dress designers. However, our *functional* health and effectiveness is related to our having enough energy in each of our ego states to be able to be appropriately *in* one or other of our ego states – in our Parent when signing a petition, our Adult when doing our accounts, and in our Child at a party.

But our healthy functioning in everyday life is more complex; if the ego states are the atoms of our functioning, their combinations are the molecules. We combine our Parent and Adult to form *judgements*, and our judgements will be influenced by both our *beliefs* (Parent) and the factual *information* (Adult) at our disposal. For example, a judge in court combines his knowledge of the actuality of the law (Adult) with his own values (Parent) before passing judgement; and barristers are aware of this in their confidence or trepidation on behalf of their clients once they know which judge is sitting on their case. 'Harsh' judgements usually imply the judge has a particularly critical Parent, 'lenient' judgements an indulgent Parent, and 'cold' judgements a leaning towards Adult.

Our Adult and Child combine to find *creative alternatives* in situations where reality (Adult) constrains the fulfilment of our wishes (Child). For example, a man whose Child yearns for a five-bedroom house on the edge of Hyde Park realises (Adult) it is beyond his means, so considers and chooses between such alternatives as a five-bedroom house in Wembley or a two-bedroom flat near Hyde Park. A bias towards Adult in setting up alternatives will tend to make the list of options 'cautious', a bias towards Child may make the options 'risky' and their achievement doubtful.

Our Parent and Child combine to form *compromises*. For example, a young woman whose Child would like to exhibit her body as a nightclub stripper compromises with her (disap-proving) Parent by becoming an artist's model. Here the collabo-ration is between two emotionally charged ego states, with no input from Adult, so in terms of actual possibilities, the individual may choose any point on the continuum from all Parent to all Child. But, of course, in terms of the psychological reality, choosing the appropriate degrees of Parent and Child is crucial in determining her sense of well-being. Too much Child in the compromise and the Parent will probably inflict guilt, too much Parent and the Child will be bitter on account of its frustration.

The most complex and significant of life's decisions, such as marriage, divorce, to have or not to have children, probably all require the harmony of all three ego states for a happy outcome to be achieved. This may account for the emphasis in traditional education – from the ancient Greeks to latter-day British public schools – on the importance of games, since these provide a singular opportunity for training the effective collaboration of all three ego states. Consider a boy playing football. His Parent is obeying the rules, his Adult skills are being exercised, and his Child is having a marvellous time!

Functional pathology arises when two or three ego states are unable to find satisfactory reconciliation of their differences, usually when two ego states are equally energised and neither will give in to the other.

When the Parent and Adult are locked in combat the individual experiences *indecisiveness*; when the Adult and Child are unable to find a solution the individual experiences *frustration* or *despair*; and when the Parent and Child are at war the individual experiences *conflict*.

Such issues are our normal experiences in life, and healthily they are resolved in a relatively short time. It is when one or other of these *impasses* become chronic that functional pathology may result. These unresolved impasses may be a new problem that crops up in our lives or an old matter from childhood that continues to affect us, either of which may be *too painful for us to face*. When we reach this point, we are inclined to cheat ourselves into feeling that there really is no problem. We force the battling ego states into a truce by providing them with *a pseudo-solution that keeps both of them quiet*. By this means *we feel better, but actually make things worse*. We achieve this by *contaminating* the relevant ego states, which is an essentially dishonest thing to do.

Consider the case of a man whose Parent ego state was taught, 'All Black people are stupid.' (Some parents give their children some pretty nasty Parent values.) But Adult reality faces this man with a highly intelligent Black neighbour – a university professor of Philosophy – whose great intelligence is an uncomfortable (Adult) fact. Now the honest thing for our man to do would be to face the discomfort of the disagreement between his Adult and Parent and allow the perceived Adult reality to amend his Parent. If he did this, he would likely form an appropriate judgement such as, 'I was brought up to believe all Black people are stupid. This is clearly not the case, so I no longer have this belief.' But renouncing our beliefs – even in the case of overwhelming facts – requires courage, and most people are more likely to attempt to bend the facts, if necessary, and cling tenaciously to their beliefs, however outdated. Our man with the Parent belief, 'All Black people are stupid', is likely to decide, 'My Black neighbour is very intelligent, but of course he's the exception that proves the rule.' This is *prejudice*.

Consider the case of a girl whose Child is in love with a man, but the man hardly knows her and certainly is not in love with her (Adult reality). The girl goes to a party where the man she loves is present. He doesn't talk to her all evening. Ideally, she would admit to herself that the man does not care for her and would decide to look elsewhere for love. But if she cannot bear to face the reality that her feelings are not reciprocated, she may interpret the situation to suit her Child wishes and say to her best friend, the next day, 'He must be in love with me or he wouldn't have ignored me the way he did last night.' This is *delusion*.

Consider the case of a woman who tries on a very expensive dress in a department store. Her Child loves it and wants it but her Parent believes she should, instead, pay the gas bill. Ideally, she would find some compromise, like buying a cheaper dress that she likes (but not quite as much as the expensive one) and can afford. But if her Child wants the expensive dress badly enough and her Parent is equally adamant that the gas bill *must* be paid, she is likely to be immobilised by her conflict. Finally, believing her Child to have won the battle, she writes out a cheque in payment for the dress and asks to have it delivered to her address. Three days later, the department store phones her and apologetically tells her that they cannot deliver the dress until she writes them another cheque, as she has put next year's date on the original one. This is *confusion*.

Contaminations are broken up by the use of the energy of the person's third ego state – the one not involved in the contamination – and another person can sometimes facilitate this. Thus, the prejudiced (Parent/Adult) man might be challenged with, 'How would you feel (Child) if someone talked about you like that?' The deluded (Adult/Child) girl might be told by her best friend, 'He's not worthy of you (Parent) and there are plenty more fish in the sea.' And the confused woman (Parent/Child) might have suggested to her, 'How about putting a deposit on it and paying for it in instalments?' (Adult)

Contaminations and their resolutions (as well as simple impasses) are intrinsic to our human nature and, dishonest as they are, need only be considered pathological when they chronically interfere with our effective or interpersonal functioning in life. But sometimes the problems in us represented by contaminations go so deep and are so painful that they are powerfully resistant to any resolution. Then the ego may resort to an even more radical device to avoid pain; the ego represses into unconsciousness the ego state(s) associated with the pain, so impasses are denied by complete evasion. Clearly this leads to a greatly impoverished personality and life. There are six different possible forms of exclusion, three exclusions of one ego state and three exclusions of two ego states. The effective exclusion of two ego states from most of an individual's daily life is the most impoverishing defence of all, and may require prolonged psychotherapy for the issues to be brought into awareness and healed.

An excluded Parent leaves a person without the necessary generalised precepts to behave responsibly or in a caring way towards himself or others. Such a person is usually perceived by others as *uncaring*.

An excluded Child makes a person lack emotional expressiveness and insight. Such a person is usually perceived by others as *joyless*.

An excluded Adult results in a chronic condition of hyper-emotionality. Such a person is usually perceived by others to be *turbulent*.

The *cold person* can be observed in the stereotype of the utterly boring scientist who insists on using his Adult exclusively to deal with all of life in order to avoid facing his unresolved Parent-

Child conflicts.

The *harsh or smothering person* is found in the stereotype of the preacher – all Parent – who metaphorically refuses to take his dog-collar off – even in bed – rather than bring Adult reality to terms with his Child fantasies. The smothering version is personified in the archetypal Jewish mother of *Portnoy's Complaint* fame.

The *infantile person* is found in the stereotype of the woman who impulsively lives the whole of her life according to the whim of the moment – all Child – rather than testing her (usually harsh) Parent against Adult reality and extracting some useful generalisations from the dialogue.

Health and pathology are also delineated in TA in the *structure* of the ego states, that is, in their contents (as contrasted with the *functional* energy flow between them). The contents of the Parent constitute our *character*; the contents of our Free Child (Natural Child plus Little Professor) constitute our *temperament*; and the totality of our Child (Natural Child plus Little Professor plus our conditioned Adapted Child) constitute our *personality*.

In any given culture there are a number of Parent values, such as truthfulness, kindness, honesty, generosity, that are generally transmitted from parents to their children. And there are probably some Parent values that are nearly universal, such as that murder and incest are wrong. Individuals will also have values and beliefs that have been familiarly taught them by their parents and others, mostly between the ages of three and six.

The totality of our Adult ego state contents is our *knowledge and skills*. Much of what an individual acquires in his or her Adult, such as literacy and numeracy, is, like the contents of his or her Parent, commonplace in a given culture, to which are added particular skills and knowledge in accordance with the child's temperament, personality, and developing interests.

But the contents of our Child, especially our Adapted Child, are much more idiosyncratic, informed as they are by the *emotional climate* of our earliest familial experiences. These experiences, which are taken on board by the child and communicated to him or her, often non-verbally, are the most powerful determiners of his or her lifelong attitudes to life. In principle, the Adapted Child attitudes that we develop are in the interests of our socialisation (such as saying please and thank-you rather than screaming for what we want) and life-preservation (such as looking both ways before crossing the road), which we need to have instilled in us long before we have a Parent ego state that can understand and justify these constraints. But our Adapted Child also contains the *unnecessary inhibitions,* transmitted by parents to their children in accordance with the neurotic components of personality that are passed from one generation to the next. As sons and daughters of Adam and Eve, we are all exiles from Paradise, and it seems to be our inescapable lot to have some hang-ups that lead us, one way or another, to chronic ways of defeating our best, more conscious attempts to find fulfilment in life.

Very often the hamartic contents of our Adapted Childs are in direct contradiction of our explicitly taught Parent ego state contents. A mother who proclaims to her daughter that being happily married is the most important thing in life (Parent) but resolutely endures her own chronically unhappy marriage will be imposing on her daughter a powerful (Adapted Child) instruction to be unhappily married. The daughter will *try* to be happily married but, however unconsciously, will almost certainly set herself up to fail in this aim. When the Parent and the Adapted Child are in conflict, the Adapted Child nearly always wins.

The hang-ups consequent on any individual's Adapted Child conditioning are ultimately unique, but over twenty years of my practice as a psychotherapist, I have discerned five basic patterns of Adapted Child defensiveness that people experience. *We all have some components of each of these structures in our lives*, but we differ from each other in their strength and hierarchy in our personalities.

The *Be Perfect* Adapted Child is the defence against the fear of death. It is dominant over all other personality types and is supremely righteous – both morally and factually – in its bid to out-control God (or the powers that be). Be Perfect is the one who always (or never) steps on the lines of the pavement and always waits for her train on exactly the same spot on the platform, and double-checks that the door is locked and all the gas taps off before she goes to bed. She is punctiliously reliable and dutiful. She is a hypochondriac and is prone to high blood pressure. Her backlash is depression.

Be Perfect is legitimised in organisation and religious observance. Moderately expressed, it is the most honourable, constructive, healthy way to live. In extremis, it dives into the most hateful and destructive syndrome of bigotry, fanaticism and murderous rage.

The *Hurry Up* Adapted Child is the defence against the fear of life. It is the least adapted of the personality types and is supremely needy of others to control its self-destructive propensities. Hurry Up is lively, spontaneous and active. He has a devil-may-care attitude to most things and is ready to do anything that promises immediate excitement. He is eager to form friendships, and is extremely enthusiastic about any new person he meets who takes his fancy. But he is equally inclined to end any relationship hysterically and abruptly as soon as the other fails to provide him with unconditional love. He is invariably late, and very accident-prone. His backlash is alienation and futility.

Hurry Up is legitimised in occupations involving speed, movement, and risk-taking. Moderately expressed, it is the most spirited, charming and adventurous attitude to life. In extremis, it is mania or paranoia.

The *Please* Adapted Child is the defence against the fear of responsibility. It is conventionally nice but sometimes very rude, obedient to win approval but also seeks to control others, through manipulation rather than overt dominance. It is Please who helps blind men and old ladies across the road, contributes her bit to charity, sends all the people she knows birthday and Christmas cards, and is generally committed to doing the right thing. She enjoys socialising and dressing and furnishing her home in as stylishly fashionable ways as she can afford. She is inclined to digestive disorders. Her backlash is being misunderstood and blamed.

Please is legitimised in hierarchical organizations in which people are both bosses and bossed, and in occupations in which a uniform is de rigueur. Moderately expressed, it is the most civilised way to live. In extremis, it is shallow, smarmy inauthenticity.

The *Try Hard* Adapted Child is the defence against the fear of failure. It is both aggressive and humbly submissive, persistent against the odds or resignedly unambitious. Try Hard is deeply sympathetic to the cause of the underdog. He is an ardent and tireless worker for the political party, usually left-wing, or any other cause that he believes in, and he uses acerbic wit to deflate the pompous and smug. But in his own interests, despite his competitiveness, he lacks confidence, is forever procrastinating, and rarely fulfils his potential. He is inclined to stress-related illnesses. His backlash is feeling an inferior failure.

Try Hard is legitimised in occupations requiring patient repetition, or where servility and some authorised aggression are combined, such as in the army or police force. Moderately expressed, it is a bravely and unrelentingly determined way to live. In extremis, it is pugilistic, get-nowhere, resentful aggression.

The *Be Strong* Adapted Child is the defence against the fear of rejection. It is uninvolved, proudly self-sufficient, brave and stoical, and always considers others' needs above its own. It is Be

Strong who leads his men into battle, is marvellous in a crisis, gets on with things, goes for brisk walks, and rises at 6 a.m. to go for an early morning swim every day of the year. He never whines or complains and (if a man) may wear a moustache to keep his upper lip hidden, just in case, despite his best efforts, it should slacken. He keeps himself healthy but is inclined to circulatory diseases.

Be Strong is legitimised in public service and in occupations that are on the receiving end of people's complaints. Moderately expressed, it is the most unselfish and sensitively considerate way to live. In extremis, it is cold, isolated, autism.

Our hang-ups and our talents are two sides of one coin. It is the human drive to find positive meaning for our inhibitions and pains that, individually and collectively, has produced all the ideas and artefacts of civilisation. I believe it is far from fortuitous that Beethoven was deaf, Monet blind, and Freud had cancer of the mouth. Without our uniquely human consciousness of self there would be no despair and no exultation.

Strokes and Transactions

Together with 'ego states', the concepts of 'strokes' and 'transactions' are what make Transactional Analysis the brilliant theory it is.

People give and receive strokes from each other every time they do or say anything that acknowledges the other's presence. Any intentional body contact made with another person is a stroke but so, too, are words and many other symbols that show we are aware of the other person. Thus a smile, a frown, a telephone call, an email, an invitation, a thank-you note or a threat are all received as strokes, as well as pats on the arm, smacks, kisses or kicks. Strokes vary in their intensity and value, from the most highly prized 'I love you' to the very slightly valued nod of recognition from a passing acquaintance.

We need strokes in our daily lives as much as we need food. And, indeed, in the earliest months of our lives we need strokes in the most basic sense of skin to skin contact in order to survive. This was definitively discovered during World War II in Paris, where there was an orphanage in which apparently well-fed and well-cared for babies were losing weight and wasting away and dying, for no discernible reason. A psychiatrist, Rene Spitz, was called in to investigate, and he discovered that the reason was that the staff were so busy feeding and keeping clean the babies in their care that nobody had any time to pick them up and cuddle them. And so it has become received wisdom that the intimate skin-to-skin contact that a baby has with its primary caretaker – usually its mother – is as vital to the baby's survival as the milk it is fed.

Rene Spitz's finding was supported by the famous experiments of the behavioural psychologist Harry Harlow who, in the 1950s, housed orphaned monkeys in a cage containing two monkey-shaped surrogate mothers: a wire mesh one to which was attached a feeding bottle, and a soft cloth one without any feeding bottle. The baby monkeys spent far more time clinging to the cloth than to the wire surrogate, and they invariably ran to the cloth one whenever they were startled by a loud noise.

In the light of this knowledge, Eric Berne, the founder of Transactional Analysis, asked himself, if physical strokes are so imperative a need in infancy, how do we manage without them once infancy is passed. He decided that we do, indeed, go on needing strokes throughout our lives, on a daily basis, in exactly the same way and as imperatively as we go on needing food. However, Berne decided, once the period of infancy is over, we learn to value symbolic substitutes for skin-to-skin contact, including any eye to eye contact we make with another human being.

The first symbolic stroke that we are capable of appreciating – and returning – is our mother's smile, when we are about six weeks old. And then, as we grow up, we learn to value a multitude of other symbolic strokes – gifts we are given, birthday and Christmas cards, invitations to parties ... We 'say it with flowers' and in innumerable other ways.

Everything that can be said about strokes is precisely analogous to what we may say about food.

Although we go on throughout our lives having our stroke needs met largely symbolically, at the deepest level of our beings, we all yearn for the nirvana we once experienced, ideally, at our mother's breasts. Loving sexual intercourse is the closest we ever get to that nirvana (ambrosia) again, and so it is the most highly valued experience that life has to offer us.

There have been some experiments performed to find out how long people can manage without any human contact (that is, strokes). In one experiment, normal, healthy adults were put in a physically comfortable situation where they had no contact of any kind with another human being, for as long as they could bear. What would you guess was the longest time that anybody could manage? After thirty-six hours there was nobody left who didn't feel they were going out of their mind (which, interestingly, is about the same length of time that most people can go without food before becoming desperate). And, as we all know, solitary confinement is the most horrible punishment that can be inflicted on people, because it is a situation in which they are completely stroke-starved. There are constitutional differences between people in how long they can survive physically without food or water, and how long they can survive psychologically without strokes, but stroke-deprivation is ultimately a sanity-threatening, if not life-threatening, situation for everybody.

All strokes are *positive* or *negative* and *conditional* or *unconditional*. Positive strokes make us feel good about ourselves, negative strokes make us feel bad about ourselves. But, quite rightly, we would rather have negative strokes than no strokes at all, just as nobody who was starving would be foolish enough to refuse a McDonald's and coke if there was no other food available. So those people who, for whatever reason, can't get positive strokes will choose negative strokes rather than none at all.

By and large, the only truly *unconditional positive strokes* people ever receive are from their mothers and fathers. And, if we are lucky, we can rely on our parents to go on loving us throughout their lives, no matter what we ever do or say. Unconditional positive strokes say, 'I love your existence. No matter what you do, I will always love you.'

Unconditional negative strokes are given instead of unconditional positive strokes to some people, even in infancy. These strokes effectively say, 'I hate you and wish you didn't exist. There's nothing you can ever do to please me or to make me love you.' Those people in the world who were largely brought up on unconditional negative strokes spend their whole lives, however unconsciously, looking for the unconditional positive strokes they were entitled to from their parents but never got. They are likely to have many self-destructive propensities and to reach out pre-emptively and with great vigour towards every new person they meet, in the hope that this is the one who will give them the infantile, unconditional positive strokes they were deprived of. They are inclined to see somebody across a crowded room and say, 'Ah, I'm in love with you. I knew, the moment I saw you, that you're the person I've been waiting for all my life,' and then the whole thing blows up in no time at all, because they provocatively test the unconditionality of the other's love with their own bad behaviour, and quickly find – of course – that there are limits to the love on offer. The hope for such people is their ability to acquire the insight to realise and accept, with rational resignation, that they are never going to get those unconditional positive strokes of which they have been deprived, but that *conditional positive strokes* are well worth having.

Conditional positive and *conditional negative strokes* are the usual strokes that are on offer in the world. For example, 'Tidy up your room and I'll take you out and buy you a new pair of jeans this afternoon' (conditional positive), or 'Do that once more and you're grounded for a week' (conditional negative).

Each individual has one or more *target positive and target negative strokes,* respectively the things we like most and the things we like least about ourselves. When we are given our positive target stroke(s) we feel great pleasure; when we are given our target negative stroke(s) we feel great pain. Target strokes, too, are conditioned in childhood. Some common positive target strokes are for looks, intelligence, generosity and sympathy; some common negative target strokes are for stupidity, selfishness, meanness and untrustworthiness.

A person's particular target strokes can be ascertained by direct questioning, such as, 'What attributes others describe you as having make you feel particularly good/bad about yourself?' but a clue to them is what kind of strokes the person tends to give to others. Thus, 'What a kind woman' is likely to be said by a woman whose own positive target stroke is kindness; 'What a mean bastard' is likely to be said by someone whose own negative target stroke is meanness.

We tend to assume that other people's target strokes are the same as our own, but in this we are often mistaken. Finding out what somebody's target strokes are, and often giving them their target positive stroke, and scrupulously avoiding giving them their target negative stroke (despite their provocation), is greatly conducive to increasing the sum total of happiness in the world. Easier said than done! Many unhappy relationships revolve around each person continually giving the other their negative target strokes.

We give and get strokes through our *transactions* with other people. Since each person has three ego states, any two people, between them, have six ego states. And when two people meet, whether or not they say anything to each other, as long as they make eye contact or touch each other in any way, they are engaged in transactions (which is just another way of saying giving and getting strokes). One person beginning to transact with another can choose (consciously or semi-consciously) to be *in* any of his or her three ego states and to address any of the three ego states of the other person. So we have nine different choices concerning the quality of the beginning transaction we initiate with another person.

It is common knowledge that about 55% of the meaning of any communication between two people is contained in visual stimuli, another 38% in auditory stimuli, including tone of voice, accent, inflexion and volume, and only about 7% in the objective meaning of the words uttered. So, with only the stimulus of printed words on a page, it is difficult to define the nature of a transaction unambiguously. Nevertheless, for the purposes of demonstration, let us assume that the essential meaning is contained in the actual words spoken, and look at an example of each of the nine ways that one person can initiate a transaction with another, even though, in principle, each statement could be said in each of the nine ways. Try saying 'What's for supper?' in each of the nine possible ways!

1   Stranger to stranger in the street: Excuse me, could you tell me the time? (Adult to Adult)
2   Boy to girl: You're the most beautiful girl I've ever met. (Child to Child)
3   Husband to wife: Shall we take the kids out for a treat this weekend? (Parent to Parent)
4   Pupil to teacher: What should I do next? (Adult to Parent)
5   Ten-year-old to his parents: You stay in bed, and I'll make breakfast. (Parent to Child)
6   Mother to whining three-year-old on the bus: We'll soon be home and then you can have some lunch and a nice rest. (Adult to Child)
7   Father to son: You'll never saw a straight piece of wood that way. Here, let me show you how. (Parent to Adult)
8   Girl to boy: You *are* clever! (Child to Adult)
9   Woman to man: Will you buy me a diamond engagement ring? (Child to Parent)

In practice, the majority of transactions between people are Adult to Adult, Parent to Parent, Child to Child, Child to Parent, and Parent to Child. Transactions between one person's Adult and another's Parent usually take place between teachers and pupils, and transactions between one person's Adult and another's Child usually take place between a grown-up and an emotionally aroused child. But it needs to be remembered that all children over the age of about six have a Parent ego state, and all grown-ups have a Child ego state. There are inevitably some transactions that have fuzzy edges, as it were, so we may not always be able to define precisely which ego state in one person is transacting with which ego state in another, although most often the diagnosis is unequivocal.

Transactions can be *complementary, crossed, or duplex.*

Consider a husband arriving home from work, and his wife observing that he has a streaming cold. How might she transact with him? She might say, from her Parent to his Child, 'You poor thing, you look full of cold. Get into bed, and I'll make you a nice hot toddy.' Or she might say, from her Child to his Child, 'Wow, you've got a corker. Keep away from me, I don't want it!'. Or she might say, from her Child to his Parent, 'I hope you're not going to go on about this cold. Remember you promised to take me out tonight.'

What might the husband's response be? To his wife's Parent to Child stimulus, 'Get into bed, and I'll make you a nice hot toddy', he might respond, 'Thank you, darling, that's just what I feel like' (Child to Parent). Or, in response to his wife's stimulus, 'Remember you promised to take me out tonight', he might respond, 'Well I'm sorry, but I'm going to have to break my promise' (Parent to Child). In both of these examples, stimulus and response together form a *complementary transaction.* That is, the ego state that was addressed responds to the ego state that addressed it, so the communication (irrespective of the feelings involved) is clear and unambiguous.

But not all transactions are complementary. Consider, for example, if, in response to his wife's Adult to Adult stimulus, 'You've got a bad cold. There's some aspirin and vitamin C in the bathroom cabinet,' the husband replies, 'Oh for goodness sake, don't you realise that once you've got a cold there's nothing you can do about it?' (Parent to Child), the transaction is *crossed.* The ego state that was addressed does not respond to the ego state that addressed it. And that particular crossed transaction, where an Adult to Adult stimulus gets a Parent to Child put-down or a Child to Parent, stop-bossing-me-about response, is probably responsible for nearly all the quarrels and wars that ever occur in the world.

There are other kinds of crossed transactions though. Any transaction that is not one in which the ego state that was addressed replies to the ego state that addressed it is technically a crossed transaction. For example, if, in response to his wife's Adult to Adult, 'There's some aspirin and Vitamin C in the bathroom cabinet', he responds Parent to Parent, 'We must get a kid-proof lock on this bathroom cabinet', he is not responding directly to what she said. Whether or not the outcome of a crossed transaction is happy is another matter, just as is so in complementary transactions, but in crossed transactions communication is handicapped by being unclear.

A particular kind of crossed transaction is an *angular* one. Consider the case of the husband responding to his wife's Parent to Child, 'Get into bed and I'll make you a nice hot toddy', with 'If you come with me' (Child to Child). This is an angular crossed transaction because the ego state that was addressed responds, but to a different ego state from the one that addressed it.

But very many of the transactions we have in our personal lives are more complex and contain *covert*, or hidden messages. These are *duplex transactions*, in which communication *nominally* takes place between two ego states (often Adult to Adult) but the real meaning of the transaction is unspoken (often Child to Child). *The covert part of the transaction is always the true communication.*

An archetypal example of a duplex transaction is in the sexual arena. A man takes a woman out for the evening, then drives her home, and when they get to her place she says, 'Would you like to come in for a drink?' (Adult to Adult). Of course we – and they

– know that the real transaction is 'Let's have sex at my place.' (Child to Child), to which the undisguised response is, 'Yeah, let's' or 'No, I don't fancy you.' (Child to Child)

Such *duplex* transactions are a very important part of civilised behaviour, especially in the sexual area of our lives, where we are all most vulnerable. To this extent, they are designed to enable us to save face as we tentatively reach out to other people, sounding out and testing the ground, especially in new relationships. In the example I have given, he is most likely to respond to her covert invitation with a covert message of his own, such as, 'Yes, I'm really quite thirsty.' On the other hand, if he responds, 'I'd love to, but I'd better get home, I've got an early start tomorrow,' his message is clear, but she is saved the humiliation of a direct rejection. Furthermore, were the man crude enough to reply to her covert invitation with, 'No, I don't want sex with you,' she could 'legitimately' reply, Adult to Adult, 'I was only inviting you for a drink.'

There is an angular type of duplex transaction, which is proto-typical of the salesman-customer interaction. Consider a middle-aged man in a clothing shop, trying on a suit, and the salesman saying, overtly, Adult to Adult, 'It's a beautiful fit, sir, but perhaps you'd prefer something not so youthful looking.' The covert transaction here is 'Buy this if you want to look younger', (Adult to Child). The salesman's aim is to 'hook' the customer's Child into the direct, overt Child to Adult response of 'I'll have it.' Should the customer see through the salesman's ploy, and be offended by it, he might, perhaps, go into his Parent and say to the salesman's Child, 'I'll thank you to mind your manners,' to which the salesman could then 'legitimately' respond comple-mentary, from his Child to the customer's Parent with, 'Oh, I beg your pardon, sir. Did I say something wrong?'

The trouble with duplex transactions is that they are also involved in all *games* (elaborated below), and it is a tightrope act for all of us to use these transactions in the name of civilisation and good manners while avoiding the mutually painful transactions that games deploy. Of course, some people will play games around the authentically well-intentioned duplex transactions of another, which is a risk the initiator takes. But some covert communication is involved in virtually all of our social and intimate encounters.

A game is a set series of duplex transactions, repetitive in nature, with a well-defined and specific 'payoff' for each of the players. A game involves each of the parties in being party to a secret position built on deception, self-deception, half-truth, or distortion of facts, or any combination of these.

When life gives us pain it is intrinsic to our human nature to maintain our righteousness and to blame others. Games speciously allow us to do this and to give and get a large number of strokes, at the high cost of a painful conclusion – our target negative stroke – at the end of the game.

There are three roles we adopt in playing games: Persecutor, Rescuer and Victim. All three roles are part of our maladaptive Adapted Child. Persecutor masquerades as controlling Parent, Rescuer masquerades as nurturing Parent, and Victim masquerades as helpless Child. We switch roles in the process of playing games, but always end in the role consistent with our own righteous bad feelings. We unfailingly spot our complementary players across the most crowded room.

'"Why don't you...? "Yes, but..."' is probably the most played game in the world. For example, a girl (Victim) phones her best friend (Rescuer) for advice about some difficult situation she finds herself in. Her friend offers her one suggestion after another – 'Why don't you...?' to which Victim consistently responds, 'Yes, but...' After some time Rescuer gets sick of this, turns Persecutor and says, angrily, 'Why bother to ask for my advice if you reject every suggestion I make?' to which Victim responds by turning Persecutor, says, 'I always knew you weren't a real friend!' and slams the phone down. The original

Rescuer ends up Victim, and the original Victim ends up Persecutor, which end result each of them has known, however subliminally, from the start. The original Rescuer may conclude something like, 'No matter how much I give to people, they never appreciate me'; and the original Victim may conclude, 'It's no good trusting people, they never give me what I want.'

We all play games sometimes – negative strokes are better than none! They are the melodrama of life, which we deem 'worth it' for the abundance of strokes we get in the process, despite the predictable conclusion.

Games are one of the six ways of 'time structuring' that Eric Berne delineated as the ways we individually choose to find an optimum balance between stroke yield and vulnerability in our transactions with others. The six ways are: withdrawal, rituals, pastiming, work, games, and intimacy, *in increasing order of stroke yield and vulnerability*. It is not so much what we are doing as how we are doing it that defines which of these ways we are structuring time. Take, for example, sex. Sex as Withdrawal is masturbatory celibacy. (No strokes, no vulnerability.) Sex as Ritual might be the Saturday night, perfunctory encounter between bored married couples. Sex as Pastiming is epitomized in the one-night-stand. Sex as Work is the domain of prostitution.

Sex as Games has multitudinous possibilities, epitomized in the 'tease' who promises but doesn't deliver. And sex as Intimacy is bilateral, candid, mutual, game-free giving and receiving of highly valued strokes, without exploitation or reservations. (Maximum stroke yield, maximum vulnerability.)

In our daily, lifelong foraging for strokes we get our calorific stroke needs met in all our activities in our own preferred balance of these six ways in which we structure our time. Analogously to the way we choose to eat, some people prefer to ingest their quota by grazing on lots of ritual and pastiming strokes, some people prefer one hearty meal of work or intimacy. But many people choose habitual game-playing as their preferred source of many strokes in return for the limited, predictable price of bad feelings, rather than ever daring to venture into the utter vulnerability as well as overwhelming satisfaction of true intimacy.

Our Species

Like all other species, our primary biologically programmed motive is to stay alive, including by the transmission of our genes to future generations. While our personal survival is an overwhelmingly powerful motive, under some circumstances we, like other species, may be seen to sacrifice our own life for the sake of the ongoing life or lives of our offspring whom we love and nurture largely by innately programmed instinct.

Like other species, our survival depends on our obtaining a sufficient continuing supply of food, good-enough protection from the vagaries of climate, avoidance of our predators, staying free of life-threatening diseases, and the avoidance of debilitating accidents that would prevent us fulfilling any of the other requirements for our continuing life.

In most respects we are unexceptional among species. Aesthetically, we lack the beauty of skin colouring or patterning of many others; we have no fur or hide or other covering that adapts us naturally to the changing seasons. We are seriously limited in the speed with which we can flee from most of our would-be predators, have little strength to do close-up battle with them; and we are nakedly unprotected by any camouflage with which so many other species are beautifully blessed. But, barring accidental, unprepared encounters with our would-be predators or with poisonous other species, our brains alone have enabled us to gain dominion over all of them.

Apart from language (See 'Languages and Theories'), we have two characteristics that distinguish us from all other species: we are anticipatorily aware of our *mortality*; and we accumulate *money and stuff*.

Like other species, when we are directly involved in warring against others' aggression towards us, we engage in fighting back, fleeing, or 'playing dead'. In these circumstances, we are so fully engaged that our fear of death is, paradoxically, over-ridden by the automatic deflection of blood from our *thinking* brains, enabling us to be fully alive – instinctively, physically – in the moment, as other species are throughout their lives. This is what motivates adrenaline-fuelled youth – especially male – to volunteer for the armed services.

For many millions of people in the world the daily struggle to find enough food (and sometimes water) similarly suffices to obliterate the fear of death in their overwhelming here-and-now struggle to stay alive.

For the fortunate few of us (throughout history) whose awareness is not wholly consumed in the immediacy of our survival needs, with full stomachs and in peace time, we need to find causes, problems and adventures that serve as displace-ments for the arousal attendant on immediate survival needs. Struggling, fighting and succeeding in overcoming our quotidian problems keeps our biological need for arousal and quiescence in a healthy flow, distracting us from facing our mortality head-on.

Happiness resides in those transitional moments of stillness consequent on food found or foe defeated, before the movement that is called being alive propels us again into an aroused state, to chase after another desire. Still contentment, epitomised in post-orgasmic lassitude, is short-lived. *Perfect stillness* is *death*.

In the *adventures* we seek out in our lives, to a greater or lesser extent, we risk life and limb in the name of being fully alive and the satisfaction of triumph that we have 'done it' and survived. The greater the risk the greater the satisfaction.

While we do learn by our own experience, even in infancy, to avoid a few quotidian pains like that of poking our finger into the flame of a candle, our ignorance of death leaves our instinctive curiosity essentially unbounded, and so demands the constant invigilation of our caretakers, who fight for our survival on our behalf, until our Parent is sufficiently developed for us to do so for ourselves.

The development of our Parent ego state provides us with an eminently important, lifelong source of our displaced need to fight for our survival: the multitudinous challenges and pains associated with our relationships, especially our sexual ones, with other members of our species. Our Parent is formed in the Oedipal stage of our development, between about three and six, when we are dragged through the turmoil of acquiring emotional literacy. In the eternal triangular battle between ourselves and our parents (and often our siblings) we acquire knowledge of love, hate, jealousy, rivalry, frustration and aggression, victory and defeat; we become bound to the resigned understanding that we cannot always have what we want. Ideally, we submit to *compromising* with others with good grace.

The end of the Oedipal stage of our development usually coincides with our first full realisation of death: one day everybody, including ourselves and our parents will cease to be – forever. This knowledge fills us with terror, against which children defend themselves with specious, comforting denial. Always, or never, stepping on the lines of the pavement, and many other kinds of obsessive rituals, revelling in violence and horror at the cinema, and playing 'bang-bang, you're dead', serve this purpose. The fulfilment of an obsessive ritual carries the 'reward' that 'nothing bad will happen', violence and murder on the screen are reassuringly 'only pretend', and in 'bang-bang, you're dead' the dead are quickly resurrected to full vitality. At this stage of development children are inclined to be usefully (to their caretakers) sensibly cautious but somewhat less 'adorable' than they were, because it is their prelapsarian innocence of the painful complexity of human relationships and of death that so charms us in the very young, and invokes in us our tenderest responses.

Then adolescence brings, with its surge of adrenaline, risk-taking that invokes stomach-churning fearfulness in our parents. But adulthood, by and large, achieves a just-right balance between safety and adventure in our lives.

While most people select body experiences for excitement: rock climbing, skiing, motor racing, riding the big dipper ... some sublimate bodily thrill-seeking into the mental realm. Intellectuals may be defined as those who choose 'mind-blowing' experiences, which are speculating on the possible invalidity of what they take for granted as truth in the realm of their favourite subject-matters. The most explicit basic training in adventurousness of the mind is offered by university departments of philosophy. There, eighteen to twenty-one year olds, emerging into the world away from their families, who have given them basic, solid sets of theories by which to live their lives, may be further educated into the (frightening) realisation that all knowledge and all beliefs are actually tenuous and 'not proven'. By being intellectually shattered they are appropriately divested of the safety of their childhood adaptations, while eventually returning to the security of their previous beliefs. However, in young adults who, for whatever reasons, do not have secure and adaptive belief systems, exposure to philosophy, I have observed, may precipitate them into a 'nervous breakdown' (severe mental injury).

By and large, both physically and mentally, we venture only a short way from our places of safety and on very strong and tethered ropes; but every now and again an irreparable injury to a person's body consequent on a physical adventure permanently changes his physical life. And every now and again an irreparable injury to a person's mind, consequent on a mental adventure, permanently changes his mental life, out of which he may even write a book!

We never fully come to terms with the meaninglessness that death makes of our mundane concerns. Some people deny death by a belief in some form of eternal afterlife, others seek continuation of their lives after physical death through being remembered for their works or deeds, and most of us find some comfort in the survival of some of our genes in our children, grand-children and further descendants. One way or another, contentment in the face of our mortality is contingent on our living life as if it has meaning, even if it doesn't.

The overwhelmingly problematic desire to find meaning in life despite our mortality has, evolutionarily, produced our Parent ego state, which other species do not have.

Like other species, we parent our young with the instinct to do so contained in our Free Child. There is evidence in other species, as well as our own, that a certain amount of Adapted Child programming is also needed for the young to become effective parents themselves. Human beings who are unloved and abused are observably handicapped in adequately parenting their own children, as is similarly the case for the young of other species who are reared in isolation, away from interaction with parents and siblings. But we human beings alone add another dimension to instinct in the rearing of our young: we teach them our beliefs, values and generalisations about life. These are the offshoots of our struggles to make the best sense we can of life. All the 'subject matters' in the world, starting with religion, but now including all of science, art, philosophy, literature, music, mathematics ... all of *culture* comprises the content of our collective Parent ego state. And that collective Parent gives us pleasure, puzzlement, enlight-enment and reassurance, and has the power to make the little interval in eternity that we call life worth living for its own sake.

Our collective Parent also mundanely protects and controls ourselves and others and compromises our bottom-line *self-preserving* impulses. In particular, the repression of many of our sexual and aggressive impulses is the price our Parent instructs us to make in the name of the (mostly) willing compromises we make between our own self-centredness and the self-centredness of others. This is what we call *civilisation*, which is a pact we make with others that effectively says, 'I will not harm you if you don't harm me. I will look after you and help you to survive when you are too young or too old or too handicapped or frail to survive without help, if you promise to do the same for me.'

Sometimes sacrificing our own Child needs and wants in favour of the 'higher' good of our Parent is cause for *pride*; sometimes selfishly giving priority to our own Child needs and wants, when our Parent believes we should not, causes us *shame*. Feeling shame is the most self-annihilating human experience and can be observed as a lifelong propensity of those who have been unloved or abused in childhood and have been given no Parent substance with which to *value* themselves. Conversely, shamelessness is abhorred. Ever since our shameful expulsion from the Garden of Eden, we have precariously walked the tightrope between narcissistic exhibitionism and self-abnegating inhibition.

Cynically, we might say civilisation does not over-ride our selfishness, merely makes it more effective in the long run. Indeed, when push comes to shove, the value of our civilised behaviour is eminently fragile. Primo Levi's testament from Auschwitz bears witness to the fact that its survivors came almost exclusively from the ranks of murderers, cheats, scoundrels and cunning con-men; those who, in ordinary life, were 'good', caring for and sharing with others, almost invariably – and quickly – perished.

Apart from our anticipatory awareness of our mortality and its attendant structures in our minds, we have one other character-istic that distinguishes us from all other species: *we accumulate money and stuff.*

The first stuff we collect is clothing. Those who live in the tropics have no need of clothing to keep them warm, and their evolved dark skin pigmentation protects them from the harmful effects of strong sunlight. But the rest of us, spread throughout the world, have a need for clothing to keep us warm and, to some extent, to shield us from too much infra-red radiation from the sun. Unlike other species, we have no fur, no seasonal moulting or other biologically given means of protecting us against the vagaries of climate. Thus, in the first place, our clothing has utilitarian value.

Like other species, we aggressively and competitively seek sexual partners. Our sexual attractiveness is an important component of our general status, our *power* in our relationships with others. Although we have some innate characteristics – beauty of face or physical form, intelligence, talents – that equip us to attract mates and to express our general status in the pecking order, our clothes also, and importantly, serve these purposes and, with artistry, enhance our natural assets and can compensate for our innate defects of attractiveness. We declare our status in our uniforms, in the fabrics with which we clothe ourselves, our jewellery, our tattoos. (In any given culture) our clothes – from rigidly prescribed and proscribed uniforms to the most bizarre and idiosyncratic declarations of individuality – communicate an abundance of information about ourselves to even the briefest glance of a stranger. Women, in particular, find a chief source of their power in their physical attractiveness; they enhance their natural assets, and hide and overcome their deficiencies of attractiveness with makeup and figure-enhancing under- and outerwear. And men, in particular, find a chief source of their power in money, the means whereby they declare to prospective mates that they have the ability to buy the finery that enhances the beauty and status of the women they choose.

But money, for all of us, is exchanged for much more than beauty and status. It is exchanged for the multitudinous varieties of stuff, entirely surplus to our survival needs, that we surround ourselves with. We go shopping – for furnishings, toys, art. We buy entertainment and holidays. Idiosyncratically, some take pleasure and pride in their *collections* – stamps, matchboxes, chess sets, vintage cars, first edition books ... – seeking out the items that will make their collections *securely 'perfect'*. Money is for all these things; money is what we want.

And yet it is a truism that money (and the stuff we exchange it for) cannot make us happy. The thrill of new purchases is short-lived. Freud explained that happiness as we ordinarily understand it resides in the delayed gratification of an infantile wish – and no infant has ever wished for money! But the illusion that money can make us happy is very resistant to disavowal, especially amongst those who do not have enough to pay for their needs, let alone their wants.

Throughout history, there have been a few exceptional individuals who have concluded that our possessions enslave rather than liberate us, and avow that the renunciation of money and the stuff it can buy is the road to contentment. A few in every age live out this credo, some going so far as to own only a loin cloth and a begging bowl, and walk freely and undefended against the limitations of the mortal coil, to which all human flesh is heir. But the vast majority go on seeking money and stuff as the raison d'être of their striving.

To the extent that money and the stuff it buys serve purposes superfluous to utility, sex and status, it seems to be a fearful addiction, a barricade, another device by which we seek speciously to feel protected against our vulnerability to disease and death. The more stuff we have, the more insatiably we want more, to fill the chink in our armour that all our stuff has so far failed to provide.

But there is one commodity that a surplus of money in our lives can buy: *time.*

In the ordinary realm of human consciousness time and its flow, from the known past and into the future is an invention as necessary in our lives as is money (or its bartering equivalent). Money and time are directly interchangeable, and there is a zero-sum relationship between them. We *spend* both time and money. Paradoxically, we are happiest when we are least aware of them.

Our experience of having more than enough as well as less than enough of either or both of them disturbs our equanimity. Optimally, we have enough of both of them to meet our survival needs and a little bit extra to play with. Each of us has an individual monetary value that we place on our time and, in everyday life, we often juggle them.

In the extreme, we are so passionately devoted to the activities in which we spend our time that an abundance of money delights us in obviating the necessity to deploy any time to merely earning enough money to meet our basic needs. But, statistically, there are very few who so enjoy their work (See 'Strokes and Transactions') that they are glad to be relieved of the 'burden' of working for money. For most people, holidays and retirement are anticipatorily enjoyed, but the loss of the strokes they daily receive – through the imposed structures of their everyday lives – quickly becomes the burden of time hanging heavily.

Duality Rules, OK

Everywhere in the universe duality reigns. It is by pairs of opposites that we apprehend the world, and find it uncomfortable.

All cultures have their myths about how unity came to be split, the myth of contemporary materialistic science being the Big Bang. To the question, What was there before the Big Bang and what caused it? scientists give the answer that there was no time before the Big Bang, so this is a meaningless question. The child in all of us knows that this is a totally unsatisfactory answer. Calling the prime cause the Big Bang still leaves the question, What made the Big Bang happen? Who made God?

Unknowing as we are, there lurks in the human psyche the notion that duality can conceivably be overcome, and a beatific state of prelapsarian oneness regained, a serene stillness that is not death. The transcendence of duality is considered the proper goal and preoccupation of life by the mystical traditions of all religions, and many religions contain within their calendars of festivals and ceremonies prescribed drug-induced high moments of release from the burden of duality.

'Good versus evil' is probably the primary symbolic duality constructed by the human mind. (See 'The Life and Death of God') While mundanely many religions see the necessity for a constant struggle for 'good' to attain and maintain its supremacy over 'evil', at their most sophisticated most religions, and many secular philosophical systems, see all opposites as actually two sides of one coin, collapsible into unity without the need for any third agent to reconcile them. Taoism in particular, in its conceptualisation of Yin and Yang avows the intrinsic *harmony rather than conflict* between opposites as the achievable perfection in ordinary life.

In the realm of psychology, from the evidence of 'idiot

savants' and my own anecdotal experience I hypothesise that there is a hard-wired intrinsic unity expressed as a zero-sum balance between above-averageness and below-averageness of a wide range of polarised abilities in every individual human being.

One philosophical duality that insistently refuses the possibility of reconciling its opposites is the mind-body dichotomy bequeathed to Western thought by Descartes, but whose validity has lately been challenged to the point of being overthrown, especially by contemporary physics and cosmology. (See 'Zeitgeist')

But like it or not duality rules our mundane lives: good and evil, up and down, left and right, hard and soft, hot and cold, night and day, male and female, being and doing, order and chaos, security and risk, caution and bravado, inhibition and spontaneity, organisation and efficiency, freedom and commitment, guilt and innocence, reward and punishment, heaven and hell, loving and hating, loving and being loved, loving and being indifferent, analysis and synthesis, self-denial and greed, penny-pinching and extravagance, self-control and self-indulgence, sureness and doubt, toughness and tenderness, depression and mania, pride and shame, extraversion and introversion, fate and free-will, meaningfulness and meaninglessness.... Opposites keep each other in check; the pull-push of pairs of opposites constitute our conceptualisation of our living experiences. There is no sound of a left-hand clapping.

Probably the closest we get to transcendence in everyday life is in passionately loving sexual orgasm; and the closest we get to a prolonged sense of transcendence is in the love we have for our children, for they do indeed form the third point of the triangle whose base line is the duality of male and female.

Duality has its base line in our biology, in our homeostatic nature which constantly swings us between arousal and quiescence. We are forever seeking the just right balance between safety and adventure in our lives. (See 'Our Species') This basic duality gets translated into a large range of experiences, which we label with thousands of different words, depending largely on context. Being aroused, when we haven't eaten for five hours becomes 'hungry', the satisfaction of which becomes 'satiated'; in response to a threatening stimulus we are 'frightened', and 'relieved' when we escape or overcome it; in anticipation of fulfilled desire we are 'excited', to the blocking of desire 'frustrated', to the unexpected blocking of desire 'disappointed'.

So pervasive are 'arousal' and 'quiescence' in everyday consciousness that they can be perceived as dominant (Adapted Child) personality traits in the makeup of individuals. I have called them the Perfectionist and the Hurrier. Their nature is elaborated in 'Personality Types', but broadly speaking the Perfectionist, consciously fearful of death, is cautious, controlled, organised and rigid. The Hurrier, aware of the pain of life, which he seeks to blot out, is fearless, risk-taking, adventurous, chaotic and agitated. These two personality traits battle it out for dominance in our personalities in the first three years of our lives as we come to terms with the vicissitudes of our physical existence in the world.

Ideally, by dint of the interaction of our (Free Child) temperament and the imposed structures of our Adapted Child, we achieve a harmonious balance between the fearful safety measures of the Perfectionist and the life-threatening excesses of the Hurrier's frenetic risk-taking.

In both the cognitive and moral education of children the appropriate balance of Perfectionist structure and Hurry Up freedom of expression has always been debated. Empirically it seems to be the case that children are best educated with a blend that gives dominance to Perfectionist structures, from the security of which they can then better manage and enjoy their forays into Hurrier spontaneity and 'creativity'. Excessive Perfectionist rigidity can be more easily remedied in later life than the insecurities attendant on excessive childhood Hurrier freedom.

Extreme dominance in any personality of either of these traits leads to two of the most painful existential experiences that beset mankind: depression and anxiety. All human beings naturally experience depression and/or anxiety from time to time in reactive response to the contingencies of life that befall them; but anybody who has experienced either in acute and/or prolonged form can testify to the overwhelming pain and dysfunction associated with them. All mundane concerns become meaningless, and the sufferer only struggles very hard to be willing to stay alive.

The (Perfectionist) experience of depression is of personal worthlessness. The sufferer is overwhelmed by her unfulfilled narcissistic needs, her movement atrophied to the point of paralysis. Nothing offered her is sufficient to convince her that her life has any value or that she has any hope of finding pleasure in being alive, although she is also terrified of death. The pain is likened to a vast space inside her body that should be filled with the love she is unworthy of.

The (Hurrier) experience of anxiety is of being pursued by a lion – all the time. The sufferer is continuously on the run, but the lion keeps chasing him and he is compelled to run faster and faster to the limit of his capacity, until death is longed for as the only way to achieve fearless quietude. The pain is likened to a knife being twisted in one's guts.

The depressed Perfectionist needs to redress the balance of her psyche by being coerced into exhilarating adventurousness and generally being active in the world, irrespective of life's ultimate meaninglessness.

The anxious Hurrier needs to redress the balance of his psyche by being coerced into rigid structuring of his daily life, giving him the security of containment that comes from order and ritual.

The natural remedy for the excesses of both the Perfectionist and the Hurrier in our everyday lives seems to be found in sleep. (I venture to suggest that being asleep is actually the default position of life; it isn't that we suffer from too little sleep but rather from too much being awake.)

In the past fifty years or so, since the discovery of Rapid Eye Movement connected to dreaming, research has revealed many complexities associated with that third of our lives we spend asleep. It is now known that REM sleep is associated with the restoration of equilibrium which has been disturbed by unresolved arousal; and REM deprivation produces increased (Hurrier) agitation. Conversely, deprivation of non-REM sleep is associated with increasing (Perfectionist) depression.

I propose that REM and non-REM sleep are the components of our biology that nightly restore our disturbed homeostatic equilibrium, physically and psychologically, between arousal and quiescence. REM sleep keeps the anxious Hurrier in us in check, and non-REM sleep refreshes us out of apathetic Perfectionist lassitude.

Barbiturates have long been prescribed for insomnia, but they reduce dreaming (REM) sleep, so the price paid for a night's sleep is increased waking (Hurrier) irritability. But depressed Perfectionists have relatively too much dreaming sleep and too little non-REM sleep, so perhaps barbiturates should be the first simple drug prescribed for depression.

In extremis and paradoxically, when the Perfectionist and the Hurrier escalate to a high enough pitch they suddenly switch from keeping each other in check to imploding in indistinguishable insanity. In their conflagration death is the only possible outcome. Witness (Perfectionist/Hurrier) religious fundamentalist suicide bombers.

More mundanely, the disease anorexia nervosa manifests the Perfectionist insanely contaminated with Hurrier self-destructiveness. Contrary to popular belief it is phenomenally rather than essentially connected to the promotion of women's sexual desirability being contingent on thinness. Under the disguise of aiming for a cosmetically sexual ideal it is actually a retreat from sexuality into the 'perfection' of childhood. Fear of eroticised adulthood is converted into a food phobia and, food being a necessity for our physical survival, it has an approximately 25% mortality rate.

I suspect the latter-day prevalence of anorexia nervosa is a maladaptive part of the Perfectionist backlash against the excesses of the Hurrier that are the hallmark of contemporary life. (See 'Zeitgeist')

We *spend* time and money (arousal), but we also *save* time and money through (quiescent) planning and effort. We each find our individualistic optimum balance between these activities (and many marital disputes involve differences on this dualistic dimension).

There is a further division of this dimension into two more sets of dualities. We each find our own preferred balance between time and money and between planning and effort.

For example, is the time saved by getting a taxi rather than a bus *worth* the extra money? Is the money I can save by buying my groceries at a distant supermarket *worth* the time it takes to get there and back instead of using my corner convenience store? How much planning of a week's menus in advance is *worth it* for the daily effort saved? How much effort in finding my way round a strange city is *worth it* for not having the bother of preliminary planning?

Thus, in our flexible responses to particular situations as well as in our habitual predispositions we balance time and money, we balance planning and effort; and then we balance the time-money outcome with the planning-effort outcome. No wonder we need to spend a third of our lives in sleep!

Broadly speaking, the cultural influence of psychoanalysis

prompts us to rationalise our neurotic propensities in terms of our imperfect relationships to our parents in childhood. The contingency of our birth order ranking is an important component of what we individually claim are the shortcomings of our upbringing. Oldest children are inclined to perceive themselves as having been denied appropriate gratification of their (Child) feelings; youngest children are inclined to perceive themselves as having been denied appropriate gratification of their (Parent) desire to be respected; and only children are inclined to perceive themselves as having been denied appropriate gratification of their feelings *and* their need for respect.

But irrespective of our rationalisations of the deficiencies in our being, we are all genetically endowed with some incipient innate handicaps and innate talents. While it should be every child's birthright to have his or her special abilities discovered and nourished and his or her handicaps helped to be overcome, in the long run it is by our own choices that we make the best and the most of the worst and the least of our potentials.

Every human being is 'above-average' in some attributes and abilities and 'below-average' in some other attributes and abilities. I profoundly believe that the number and extent of our handicaps and talents has nothing whatsoever to do with the happiness we experience in life.

Our hang-ups and our talents are two sides of one coin. It is the human drive to find positive meaning for our inhibitions and pains that, individually and collectively, has produced all the ideas and artefacts of culture and civilisation. Thus a child who had a scarringly painful family life may heal herself through becoming a welfare officer or a psychotherapist; a stammerer an orator; a deaf child a teacher of the deaf; a child with a facial blemish a beautician or plastic surgeon.

It is the people who know themselves to be handicapped in some way – physically or psychologically – and are passionately committed to healing their own wounds (and in the process healing others) who often experience the deepest possible satisfaction with life.

When all is said and done the balance of our abilities and disabilities may be a necessary physiological duality, as evidenced in the fascinating existence of idiot savants, those severely mentally retarded people who also have particular talents incredibly greater than even the most intelligent of the rest of us. Their special ability is usually in arithmetical calculations, such as faultlessly and nearly instantaneously naming the day of the week of any date, past or future; or of precisely knowing the number of jelly beans in a jarful of them. Some have the equally incredible ability to observe a cityscape for a few seconds and then reproduce it as a drawing, accurate to the minutest detail.

What is the connection between these people's handicaps and talents? Could the rest of us gain these (or other) talents by forfeiting part of our normally functioning abilities? Is there a zero-sum equation between all our abilities and disabilities and, if so, how many such dimensions are there, and how are they represented in the anatomy and physiology of our brains?

Apart from the birth of a child, there are few occasions in life where we are gratuitously gifted with moments of joy that override the bounds of mundane duality. I had one such experience on August the 11th 1999 when I stood, with about 20,000 other people, on Plymouth Hoe and witnessed the first total eclipse of the sun for seventy-two years that was visible from mainland Europe. The shops all closed; the darkness-triggered street lighting was switched off. As in days of yore, young and old, poor and rich, educated and ignorant became for a moment as one in response to the majesty of the cosmos.

The weather being overcast (as it so often is in England) and our human eyes being so cleverly adaptive, until the actual totality the physical experience was merely of a very gloomy day.

But at 11.18 a.m. – exactly as predicted! – we were plunged into blackness and a roar of transcendental joy burst forth from 20,000 mouths. For that moment all separateness between people was lost and Man and God were reunited. Not since the moon landing had I witnessed such a beautiful moment of humanity united in spiritual awe.

Realities

All human beings, from the moment they are born and throughout their lives, have two basic needs: *to get strokes and to make sense of the world and themselves in it.*

Most parents instinctively give their babies all the tender, loving *physical strokes* that are so vital to their well-being, and most babies grow and thrive. A contented baby held lovingly in its mother's arms is often depicted as the epitome of bliss and, in the deepest unconscious part of our Child, this is the state of being we all long to return to.

In reality, of course, this nirvana can no longer be had once infancy is past. The closest we get to it again is in *loving sexual intimacy* which, for most grown-ups is the most sought-after and fulfilling of all possible experiences. But even this is not enough. Our stroke needs are continuous and imperative throughout the whole of our lives and even people passionately in love cannot fulfil *all* of each other's stroke needs. All of us, in fact, get most of our stroke-needs met by symbolic substitutes for actual physical contact; any acknowledgement of our existence by another human being is counted as a stroke, although the calorific value to us of the strokes we receive varies, from the only slightly valued nod and 'good morning' by a passing acquaintance to the highly prized 'I love you'. Getting our daily need for strokes fulfilled is as imperative to our wellbeing as fulfilling our daily need for food. Stroke-deprivation is as discomfiting as hunger for food.

We would rather get negative strokes – an angry word, a spit in the eye, a kick in the shins – than get no strokes at all; just as the most health-conscious of us would rather have a Big Mac and a coke than no food at all. Negative strokes keep us going even though we can easily become habituated to them (as to unhealthy food) and do ourselves long-term harm. People – children in particular – who chronically seek negative strokes are often (stupidly) assessed as 'just looking for attention'. We are all looking for attention (strokes) all the time. Those habituated to seeking negative strokes are the unhappy people who are unable to find enough positive ones to sustain them.

Thus we are deeply dependent on interaction with our fellow human beings. We vary constitutionally in the amount of stroking we need to maintain our wellbeing. But, with the very rare exception of hermits, none of us can manage without some regular human intercourse.

The other characteristic that we are pre-programmed for is to make sense of our experiences, from the moment we open our eyes on the world as neonates.

At first, we infer, the newborn baby has only the single inchoate experience of the world as a buzzing, whirring confusion. He is unable to distinguish between 'self' and 'not-self'; he and the universe are one.

The existence of our sense organs determines that we cannot avoid being constantly bombarded with facts, and our physical and psychological survival in the material world and the world of people necessitates our collecting and interpreting clusters of facts into theories, which become the truths by which we live our lives. Though the number of facts in the universe is infinite, once we have experienced and interpreted into truth a sufficient number of facts about matters pertaining to our survival, in the context of our personal environments, we stop.

Thereafter, our minds filter out the information received by our sense organs that is irrelevant to or contradicts the theories we have formulated. All stimuli that do not confirm the conclusions we have already arrived at, conclusions that reassure us of our *security* in the world, are rejected by our brains as 'white noise' and unnoticed by our conscious minds.

So step by step, to the delight and awesome wonder of most parents, through the use of the hard-wired faculties of his brain, the baby begins to *know things*. By about a month he can focus his eyes and a single object can be seen by him as separate from everything in his field of vision. By about six months of age he clearly demonstrates that he knows the difference between 'self' and 'not self'; he can reach for and drop an object and cry for it when it is out of reach. And from this time onward his knowledge of the physical realities of life increases by leaps and bounds. He learns that if his body comes into too rapid or forceful contact with an object 'it hurts'. He learns that hot things hurt, too. He learns that 'what goes up must come down'. He learns that some things are heavy and some things light and that some things too heavy to lift can be moved by horizontal force. He learns that an object on wheels can be given added momentum with friction and that objects vary in their fragility. Until, by about the age of four, his *practical knowledge of physics* is virtually complete.

Alongside all the knowledge he gains in these few years about *physical reality* he acquires an equivalent amount of *knowledge of psychological reality*. At about six weeks of age he knows that human faces bring him pleasure, and he proves he knows this with a stroke-inducing smile. By about two months of age he knows his mother's face as distinct from all faces as promising the most strokes of all, and by about seven months he probably responds to the *absence* of his mother with terror. He is beginning to experience what stroke-deprivation means. By about nine months his Little Professor knows cunning ways to get attention – strokes – if they are not forthcoming, such as by a manipulative cute smile or by banging his spoon on his high-chair tray when his mother is paying attention – giving strokes – to someone other than himself. Until, by about six years of age, with all his ego states now formed, from his experiences of family life he *knows* all the essentials of psychological reality – *that is, the meaning of strokes and how to get them.* By about the age of six, to all intents and purposes, our minds are closed, and every experience we subsequently allow ourselves to have is a recapitulation, literally or metaphorically, of evidence for the truths we have established.

If, by dint of some innate incapacity or inadequate input from the environment, we are unable adequately to filter the virtually infinite number of stimuli that bombard us, we are deemed *mad*. Two well-known forms of madness that are associated with the brain's malfunctioning filtration are schizophrenia and autism. In schizophrenia the individual is overwhelmed with consciousness of more stimuli than his brain can process coherently; in autism the individual has filtered out so much that there is not enough left to formulate actionable understanding of human interactions.

Although the six-year-old has only a very limited capacity for expressing in *words* (either in her own mind or in talking to others) what she knows about the world and about human relationships, by the evidence of her *actions* she already has vast stores of information and wisdom. Indeed, not only six-year-olds but all grown-ups, too, are rarely self-conscious of all the learning we once had to do that enables us now to manage our lives at even the simplest levels.

In our ways of looking at objective reality we are all very much alike. We differ from each other to the extent that we each have our own ways of perceiving that highlight some, and gloss over other, aspects of reality. Thus an artist may tend to see 'nothing but' colours and shapes, a banker will focus on the economic aspects of reality, and a naturalist may find city streets 'empty'.

Nevertheless, allowing for the differences of focus that are conditioned by differences of interest, by and large we have all been taught to interpret the world in ways that all sane people call 'correct'.

Consider, for example, a conversation between a five-year-old and his or her mother.

Five-year-old: Mummy, why won't my ball stay up?

Mother: Because everything falls back to the ground.

Five-year-old: Why?

Mother: Gravity makes everything fall down.

Thus 'gravity' becomes an explanatory truth in the child's mind.

I remember one of my daughters, then aged four, asking me, 'Mummy, why are all the big aeroplanes at the airport and all the little ones in the sky?' to which I was obliged to reply,

'The ones in the sky are really big, too. They just look little because they are a long way away.'

I recall feeling some poignancy that, in my reply, I was closing my daughter's mind to all other metaphysical possibilities in which, for example, the aeroplanes at the airport could be deemed *really* little, but only look big because they are so close. Thus, in the name of sanity, *we close our children's minds* to all but the agreed conventions by which we explain the nature of our perceived realities. Each answer we give a child to the questions she asks about the nature of the world, makes the world, for her, a more *predictable* place. She *knows* a bit more and feels that much more secure. (Who has not, at some time, found gratification, however small, in testing the security of our knowledge about the world by actions, for example, like covering a burning candle with a glass and 'proving' – again – that, yes, fire does need a continuous supply of oxygen to go on burning?)

But our minds are not completely closed.

Firstly, facts incompatible with our scientific beliefs may insistently refuse to go away. When its time has come, a new idea will be heard, and scientific reality is extended or transformed. Individuals, too, may rarely have mind-blowing experiences that permanently alter their deepest theories of reality. And, in small ways, creative thinkers of all kinds discover solutions to their disease with the way things are. (I define creativity as the outcome of the struggle to reconcile desire (Child) with reality (Adult).)

Secondly, we all desire to experience again the excitement of our earliest years before we had yet chosen the life-preserving truths we would live by. For this, we flirt with death – physically or mentally – from the thrills of engaging in dangerous sports to courses in philosophy that challenge us to re-constitute reality from first principles.

So, step by step, we accumulate in our Adult ego states the thousands of bits of information about the world that we all share. After infancy it is not only our mothers and fathers who give us all this information. From the time we start school – at the latest – books and teachers and television and other children provide additional ways of satisfying our continuing quest to *know things*. Through the increasing diversity of our sources of information, the older we get the more different we become from each other in the totality of what we know. Our interests become more particular, and we get to know about some things in very great depth and detail while being satisfied to know little about other things. But the most basic facts about the world – facts that are most important for us to know in order to feel secure in everyday life – are the same for all of us and were learnt at our mother's knee.

Most of the time we take for granted the everyday effectiveness our knowledge gives us, calling it 'instinctive'. Only structural engineers, in their everyday working lives, may need to be fully aware of the laws of physics; and only osteopaths need, in their working lives, to know all the bones in our bodies. Yet all normal people respect the law of gravity, know the dangers of cars, electric sockets and fires, can cut their own toe nails, adroitly handle a knife and fork and ... a thousand and one other things which once, long ago, before they learned them, they did not understand and could not do.

In exactly the same way and in order to fulfil the same basic need to make sense of the world so as to feel *secure* in it, we learn about psychological reality. Learning about physical reality enables us safely and confidently to interact with *things*, learning about psychological reality enables us safely and confidently to interact with *people.*

All the time we are asking our mothers and fathers about gravity and temperature, animals and birds, night and day, sand and snow ... the multitudinous physical realities that impinge on us, we are also asking about men and women, life and death, love and hate, anger, jealousy, ownership rights and sharing, happiness and unhappiness, good and bad, reward and punishment ...

And so, by the time we first leave home to go to school, we are basically equipped to get our stroke needs met in the world at large.

Much of our psychological knowledge is ritualistic, rigidly ingrained in our Adapted Child and supported by our Parent morality, such as saying 'hello' and 'goodbye', 'please' and 'thank you', looking both ways before crossing the road, controlling our impulses to kick, push, spit or shout at other people in order to get what we want, and generally being obedient to the Golden Rule. Such ritualistic knowledge about effective interactions with other people is, for most people, experienced as automatic and 'instinctive'.

However, we all make one huge, early mistake – a mistake that most people continue to make for the rest of their lives. *We presume that just because everybody else's physical reality is the same as our own, so everybody else's psychological reality is the same as our own. It isn't.*

True, there are often large areas of overlap between one person's and another's psychological realities, or else we would continually fail to get strokes from other people. But the truth – however uncomfortable – needs to be faced, that unhappy relationships arise because each person's stroke needs and learnt ways of getting his stroke needs met are often incompatible with the stroke needs of particular others. What we witnessed and were told about people in our early family life may be very different from what our best friend witnessed and was told about in his family. Some families are generally amiable, some sad, some angry and quarrelsome, some loving, some rejecting, some quiet, some noisy, some organised, some chaotic, some stable, some changeable. It is on the basis of the characteristics of our own particular family that each of us decides, idiosyncratically, what human nature and life are all about. We carry these decisions with us for the rest of our lives.

One child becomes the man whose greatest happiness is his close and loving family life, his greatest difficulty in life being his constant worry about money. Another becomes renowned in his field of work and feels immensely rewarded by the honours heaped on him, but constantly does battle with his inclination to alcoholism. One woman is constantly appreciated for her femininity and beauty but feels inferior for never having completed her secondary schooling, while another is profoundly positively stroked as a mother but miserable as a wife.

For the good and the bad in our lives, what is *relevant* to one person is *irrelevant* to another. Wealth versus poverty, health versus illness, fame versus anonymity, faith versus doubt, intelligence versus stupidity, beauty versus ugliness, security versus adventure are some of the commoner dimensions to be found in people's psychological make-ups.

Broadly speaking, we might say that in our understanding of physical reality we are all about ninety percent alike and ten percent divergent; in our understanding of psychological reality we are about ten percent alike and ninety percent divergent. It is the convergences and divergences of one person's and another's psychological realities that are responsible for all the pains and all the joys in our relationships.

But irrespective of the variability of our learned psychological knowledge, whatever that knowledge is, it enables us – with greater or lesser happiness – to fulfil *our underlying need to experience life as orderly and predictable.* So, by the time a child is about six years old his basic personality (Child) and character (Parent) are complete, and his Adult has also acquired a vast array of knowledge and skills concerning his interactions with the objective, material world. His ego states are differentiated and available for their appropriate uses; experientially, he is aware of his and others' fundamental need for strokes; he moves about comfortably in the physical world because he knows enough about it to be confident of the *predictability of events* in response to his actions; and he moves about comfortably in the psychological world – at least within his family – because he knows enough about *how to get strokes* to make sure this most vital of his needs is fulfilled.

Some years ago the variability of people's stroke habits was made vivid to me in an encounter I had with the members of one of my therapy groups. It was a few days before Christmas, when I walked into my living room, in which the group was already assembled, and I heard one group member saying to another, 'Thank you very much for your Christmas card. Um, um, we're not sending any this year, but I hope you don't think we're ungrateful,' and I realised she was giving herself her target negative stroke – ingratitude. That situation, bumping into somebody who has sent you a Christmas card when it's too late to send them one – no big deal, but we've all experienced it and been inclined to have some, however mild, uncomfortable feeling.

So I took advantage of this situation and said, 'Okay everybody, it's December the twenty-third and you bump into somebody who has sent you a Christmas card, and you haven't sent them one. Quickly and spontaneously tell us how you feel.'

We got 'guilty', 'embarrassed', 'worried', 'ungrateful', 'ashamed' and 'selfish', but what was most fascinating were the looks of amazed disbelief on people's faces as others declared their target negative strokes, as if to say, 'That's not the feeling you're supposed to have.' There was silence at the end, which was broken by one of the 'guilty' ones turning to the 'ungrateful' one and saying, 'But you do feel guilty for being ungrateful, don't you?' And the 'ungrateful' one said, 'No I don't.'

Different strokes for different folks!

The 'nature versus nurture' issue has been largely transcended by the unravelling of the human genome and the recently developed subject of epigenetics, which testifies to the complex interactions between genes and environment, from the womb onwards throughout life. The presently received view is that there are undoubtedly environmental conditions (especially in the formative years of childhood) which can and do modify our genetic programming, such as the increased height attained by recent generations of children through improved nutrition. But, by and large, we accept that there are actually very narrow limits written into our genetic inheritance, beyond which no environmental factors are likely to be effective. We accept that we cannot change our individually inherited physical characteristics, such as the colour of our eyes or our fingerprints; nor can we do much about our collectively inherited characteristics such as when, within quite narrow limits, we will get our teeth, reach puberty, go grey, and die.

Environmentalism probably achieved its zenith in the 1970s in association with the Women's Liberation movement. Then it was fashionable to espouse the primacy of nurture even in gender distinctions. It was argued that if only we gave little girls toy cars and little boys Barbie dolls it would be apparent how little difference there innately is between the sexes. One almost incredible story that arose out of this insane politicisation of gender at that time was of a baby boy whose circumcision went seriously wrong and his genitals were left deformed. The *surgeon* advised the mother to bring the child up as a girl, which she did. At the age of thirty-five *he* (the supposed girl) committed suicide, at which time his tragic story came to light.

Psychoanalysis does not, of course, make any such ridiculous claims about the power of nurture over nature, but it does make the modified claim that our personalities and characters are overwhelmingly determined by our earliest conditioning; and all humanistic schools of psychology bear some allegiance to this position.

My own view is that our earliest remembered experiences are *as if* principal causes of what we become; that is, our brains selectively remember (and even, as in our birth stories, sometimes create) those events that concur with our genetic predisposition to construe our experiences in the ways we do. (See 'Languages and Theories') Witness siblings' often very different memories of shared family experiences as well as the very different interpretations they may each give to memories they do share.

But it doesn't matter if the environmental events of our early years are not 'really' causes, but are subsumed to the deeper determinism of our genetic inheritance which, in turn, may be subsumed to an even deeper cause, to karma or whatever, until we stop and call the 'final cause' God (or unified field theory).

Languages and Theories

All 'truths' and all languages are created by the human mind; all theories about anything and everything may be thought of as different but concordant languages.

Language is an attribute which is unique to human beings as a species. Animals often make use of signs, which point to what they represent, but only the language of human beings makes use of arbitrary and conventional symbols.

Because the emergence of language is located so far back in history, there are no direct historical traces, and there is no general agreement on its ultimate origin or age. Hypotheses concerning the origin of human language abound, but none has yet received consensual endorsement. Some hypotheses suggest that human language began as a collection of signs, such as are used by other species, and only gradually evolved into its eventual, symbolic complexity; others suggest that it was created by conscious invention and was singularly human from the start. But one thing linguists agree on is that there are no existing 'primitive' languages; all modern human populations speak languages of at least comparable complexity and expressive power.

Within very broad limits, any language is capable of expressing any thought that any human being may wish to utter. From China to the Azores we are all one species. However, environmental conditions, both physical and psychological, have created differences in the relative importance and pertinence of various elements in different peoples' experiences of life. And these differences are reflected in the vocabulary of any given language-culture. A centrally important issue will have invoked the creation of minutely discriminating words to match the need to perceive such differences. Thus, we are told the Inuit have many words for our one word 'snow'; and the few words of

Yiddish I know enable me to describe varieties of fools with subtlety and gusto.

Although we will each, inevitably, be most fluent in our native tongue, a degree of multi-lingualism in the form of appropriate interpolations of foreign words and phrases can do nothing but enrich with nuances our experiences and our expressiveness.

Inasmuch as spoken language serves interpersonal communication (which has immediate survival value), it seems likely that this was the first existent 'theory' created by the human mind, and this was probably succeeded next by some sort of graphical representation that evolved into written language. And then followed all the theories of the multitudinous symbolic subject-matters which today furnish the vault of collective human consciousness.

It is unlikely that the total span of recorded history has been a long enough time for evolution to have wrought any noticeable changes in human nature. Whenever and wherever people have recorded their reflections on the problems inherent in human beings' relationships with each other and the universe the same difficulties and perplexities are met with the same solutions and wisdoms over and over again.

'There is nothing new under the sun' and those people we call original thinkers usually utter old truths in a new voice which is better attuned to the tone of their time. Copernicus revived the Greek idea of a sun-centred universe; Darwinian evolutionary theory had been espoused by various others since before the common era; the Unconscious had its place in literature long before Freud; and the ideas expressed by Ovid two and a half thousand years ago are as popular in replies to the lovelorn in today's magazines as they ever were. Apples falling on people's heads and causing uniquely revelationary moments in human thought are a romantic myth.

Nevertheless, theories about everything come and go, have

their day, and are discarded as newly observed 'facts' force us to supersede our current theories with more comprehensive or radically different theories that will accommodate the new facts as well as the old. All theories are 'true' until such time as they will not bend to some data that refuses to be ignored. Then the theory must be elaborated or replaced.

Theories are ways in which human beings make sense of their observations. Theories provide us with security by enabling us confidently to predict the outcome of the collision of our bodies and minds with the material world and with other people. From the moment we open our eyes on the world as newborn babies we begin to theorise, and we continue to do so for the rest of our lives.

In our first few years of life our very physical survival as separate human beings depends on our successfully formulating a very large number of theories at a very rapid rate. In our early months and years of life, because our unknowingness makes us so vulnerable, Nature has endowed us with an abundance of curiosity as a special device for fulfilling our urgent mission to survive physically and psychologically in the face of all the complexities we encounter. Not only do we passively receive and ruminate on all the stimuli that bombard us unbidden but, by voluntary exploration, we actually invite the world of things and people to collide with us and make even more abundant the data we are bound to synthesise into theory.

By and large we have each formulated all our essential theories about the nature of the world, our own existence, and the nature of our relationships with others by the age of about six. Thereafter, some baroque flourishes may be added to the basic structure of our achieved frames of reference but, to a large extent, our minds are now closed, and every experience we subsequently allow ourselves to have is a recapitulation – literally or metaphorically – of 'evidence' for the truths we have established. (See 'Realities')

However, our minds are not completely closed, either individually or collectively. It happens from time to time, that facts incompatible with our established theories refuse to be ignored, and we are *forced* to accommodate them in our minds, however uncomfortable and frightening the process. Once in a while in human history the collective mind is assaulted by an Einstein who challenges the profoundly held 'certainties' of a Newton. Although, at first, we fight tooth and claw to resist the new fact – with derision, ridicule, inquisitions, and any other weapons we can muster – in due course, when its time has come, an idea *will* be heard, 'truth' adjusted to accommodate it, and it becomes the basis of a new orthodoxy until the vagaries of a determinism beyond our understanding deem it, too, to have had its day.

In the lives of individuals, also, contingencies may rarely seem to arise from nowhere that force us, partly or wholly, to reformulate our meanings-of-life. And from the testimonies of those individuals whose truths have been resoundingly shattered, forcing them to create new theories to live by, the precipitating experience seems nearly always to be one in which they nearly died in physical actuality, or else suffered extreme trauma, such as being forcibly incarcerated or brainwashed, so that they nearly died psychologically. It takes a mighty force to make us give up our 'certainties'!

However, our overwhelming, self-preservative quest for certainties by which to live our lives is balanced by our quest for excitement. (See 'Our Species') People vary in the balance of their needs for security and adventure, but curiosity – which is tantamount to aliveness – leads us all, from time to time, to seek out risky uncertainty by which to capture again the excitement of early childhood when we 'knew' so little and our survival still depended on the loving watchfulness of our caretakers.

Many people select body experiences for such excitement: rock climbing, skiing, motor racing, riding the big dipper ... Intellectuals may be defined as those who choose 'mind-blowing' experiences, which are speculating on the possible invalidity of what they take for granted as truth in the realm of their favourite subject-matters. The most explicit basic training in adventurousness of the mind is offered by university departments of philosophy. There, eighteen to twenty-one-year olds, emerging into the world away from the sanctuary of their families, who have given them basic, solid sets of theories by which to live their lives, may be further educated into realising that all knowledge and all beliefs are actually tenuous.

Our truths are like balloons which contain the facts we breathe into them until they are stretched to their limit and burst. As each balloon bursts we start to blow up another, for we need our minimum number to clutch to avoid being sucked into the annihilating vortex of the ultimate Black Hole.

The separate balloons in our particular clutch exist compatibly but unrelatedly to each other, one or other being 'best' for the particular purpose of a given moment. Accordingly, there is, for example, no such thing as the 'correct' definition of the table in front of me. It can equally validly and comprehensively be defined in terms of its physical properties, its chemical composition, its functional qualities, its colour, its shape ...Thus the more balloons we have the greater our versatility in our responses to the 'facts' of our lives.

Yet we all long for one huge, unburstable balloon that will contain us and all our small balloons, but which will also exclude all Black Holes. Some people find this balloon and call it God; others are still seeking it in a mathematical formula they call Unifying Field Theory. (See 'The Life and Death of God')

For those who thrill to the excitement of theorising anew, there is no age at which it needs to stop. Theorising is proportional to curiosity and goes far beyond the demands of biological necessity. Although curiosity may justifiably diminish with age, as fewer and fewer events are unprecedented in the life of the individual, for those of us with a continuing appetite for mental excitement, the possibilities are endless – from jigsaw puzzles to cosmology, for the child within us all.

In order to theorise we collect facts and categorise them. Categorising is the primary function of the human brain in making sense of anything and everything. Our subject-matters lead us to create and codify the categories into which we wish to sort our relevant facts.

Some categorisations of people and ideas and things are discrete, and some are sub-sets of wider categorisations we have already made. Which discrete categories we apply and how far we go in refining any of our categories into sub-categories depends on the context in which the person, idea or thing is being described. 'Men' is sufficient in the context of public lavatories; 'female, teenager, size 10' is sufficient for a clothes manufacturer; 'intelligent, moderate socialist' may be sufficient in the context of a trade union election. So it goes on, to the limiting case of a beloved other whom we wish to describe, and thus know, down to the tiniest freckle of his or her physical and psychological being.

Categorising ourselves and others psychologically piques our vanity because it reduces the significance of the exceptional characteristics in ourselves in which most people take such pride. But in categorising ourselves and others by means of theories that are appropriately deep and comprehensive we enlarge our awareness of the samenesses and differences between people, adding a dimension of objective understanding to our emotional reactions to events and to other people. It is commonly received wisdom that, in judging others, the more like us they are the more accurate our assessment of them is likely to be; and unless we categorise people, we implicitly take all of our own characteristics to be the human norm, and we discount the validity of all the characteristics of other people except those that are also our own. Understanding the dynamic meaning of our own type in relation to the known type of another individual enables us to please that individual with finesse, especially by giving them their target positive strokes (See 'Strokes and Transactions'), and also enables us most effectively to defend our vulnerabilities against the assaults of that individual. Categorising people psychologically enlarges our humanity and increases our tolerance of ourselves as well as others. For the price of foregoing some of our narcissistic allegiance to our intrinsic uniqueness, we gain a corresponding diminishment of shame for our short-comings, which we can now accept as 'only human'.

We are holograms. Given enough attention, any part of us can be seen to be representative of our wholeness. Palmistry, iridology, graphology, physiognomy, reflexology, astrological sun-signs, homeopathy, acupuncture, psychological typologies, blood groupings, phrenology, national stereotypes, socio-economic groupings, biochemistry, anatomical types, kinaestheology, enneagram types ... all bear witness – some more successfully than others – to our instinctive appreciation of our holographic nature. All that is required is a prolonged concentration on some sign to evolve a coherent, holistic theory. A four foot six inch tall man who was also, briefly, something of a television celebrity, avowed that he had constructed a reliable personality typology out of his perception of the shapes of people's nostrils!

Body and mind, nature and nurture are inextricably entwined as the determinants of our achieved wholeness. But for each of us there is an essence which all our theories seek to isolate and understand.

We are metaphorical and symbolic creatures, and some of our deepest individual truths are discoverable through universal metaphors. Ask anybody the following questions to reveal some of their deepest idiosyncratic realities. Reveal yourself to yourself by answering the questions before reading the interpretative key.

1) In a few words, describe your favourite animal (or bird or fish). 2) In a few words describe your second favourite animal (or bird or fish). 3) In a few words describe the sun. 4) In a few words describe the sea.

1) reveals our self-perception. 2) reveals our ego-ideal (and often describes the kind of people we are drawn to love). 3) reveals our present and/or childhood perception of home. 4) reveals our truth about sex.

The beauty of these questions is that they can be asked without impropriety and answered without embarrassment between complete strangers as well as intimates, yet they provide, in a jiffy, deeply useful knowledge of the potential for relationship between us.

Some memorable answers I have received to these questions include: a bisexual man for whom the sea is 'variable'; a man whose favourite creature was a cat and whose second favourite was a canary; and a lesbian woman whose favourite animal was a cat and whose response to the question of her second favourite creature was, 'I can only think of cat.'

Another interesting way in which people reveal themselves is through the stories of their births. It is strangely true that what we remember being told about our births (or our mother's pregnancy with us) are precise metaphors for the general quality of our stroke experiences in our relationships. However, what people remember being told, I have found, does not always correspond to the independent testimony of a grown-up child's parents. It seems we *create our birth stories to match our achieved ways of experiencing others.*

'I know nothing about my birth' usually means, 'I have no understanding of how I relate to other people.' 'I/my mother nearly died,' means 'I/other people experience great distress in relationship to me.' One woman who reported, 'When my mother was pregnant with me she could eat hardly any foods, but the few she could eat she loved,' confirmed that she doesn't like most people but has a few very loving relationships. And a paranoid schizophrenic told me, 'When I was born they held me upside down. I cried and they laughed.'!

Man is a symbolic, metaphorical being. All languages are full of universally understood metaphors that express wisdom accumulated by humanity over aeons of time. Language itself may be thought of as the ultimate metaphor for our experiences and is that which distinguishes us from all other species and gives us dominion over them.

Five Personality Types

Over twenty years of my practice as a psychotherapist I have developed, inductively from observation, five distinct Adapted Child personality types. They are the ways by which, in the name of Parent values, they lead us, through playing games and deploying the inauthentic roles of Persecutor, Rescuer and Victim, to achieve our target negative strokes and associated negative existential views of life.

I have given the types the names of their pseudo-Parent values: Be Perfect (Perfectionist), Hurry Up (Hurrier), Please, Try Hard and Be Strong. We all use each of them sometimes, but we are different from each other in their hierarchy in our personalities.

At first, my presumption was that, for health, we need to 'get rid of' these inauthentic devices and contents in our Adapted Childs, but I came to realise that, as well as representing our 'hang-ups', they also contain some of our virtues and incipient talents; they need to be transformed rather than eliminated.

Ultimately, of course, each of us is unique, but for much of everyday life broad brush strokes are sufficient in our bids to understand and communicate effectively with our fellow human beings.

As well as in our achieved grown-up personalities, each of the types is characteristically associated with universal stages of child and adolescent development.

The battle between Be Perfect and Hurry up is particularly associated with the first three years of life as we come to terms with existence itself. Please, Try Hard and Be Strong are associated with our learning how to give to and get strokes from other people.

There is a propensity to Please behaviour in the years between one and three when the Adapted Child is at the height of its formation, to which Try Hard and Be Strong are added in accordance with our familial experiences in the Oedipal stage of development between three and six.

Be Perfect and Be Strong tend to be dominant orientations of the child in latency, between about six and twelve, in response to the child's first realistic awareness of death; puberty brings Hurry Up freneticness to the fore; and adolescence is a notably competitive Try Hard stage of development as we fight for our self-esteem against the 'superiority' of our parents.

In this essay I will outline the nature of the five basic personality types. (A comprehensive account of them is contained in my book *Pain & Joy in Intimate Relationships*.)

Be Perfect is the defence against the fear of death. All our fears are derivative from the fear of death, and once this fear is dissipated, anything is possible. But the most lasting accomplishments of mankind are the outcome of developed Be Perfect through which we make our bid for a little bit of immortality.

Be Perfect is the religious view of life. Religion represents the accumulated wisdom of mankind about how we can live most contentedly in the face of our knowledge of our mortality. All religions offer us rewards for self-discipline and stoicism accepted in the name of a cosmic Will and knowledge and meaning beyond our capacity to comprehend fully. People who are predominantly Be Perfect live life religiously, whether they are adherents of the orthodoxies of one of the named religions or only of their own idiosyncratic, self-created, self-imposed order and rigid disciplines, by which they hold at bay their fear of death and give 'meaning' to their lives. Without a basic minimum of Be Perfect we would each kill ourselves by accident in a very short time.

As a personality type, Be Perfect is a close relative of the psychoanalytic obsessive-compulsive syndrome. It is associated with any too great or too rigid structuring of everyday life in childhood. It is generally a safe hypothesis that anyone with a Roman Catholic or Jewish background, even if lapsed, or anybody brought up strictly in any other faith, has Be Perfect as his or her favourite or second favourite Adapted Child syndrome. Be Perfect is the one who always (or never) steps on the lines of the pavement and always waits for her train on exactly the same spot on the platform, and double-checks that the door is locked and all the gas taps off before she goes to bed. She is punctiliously reliable and dutiful.

Overall, Be Perfect is manifestly superstitious, critical, intolerant, righteous, nit-picking, moralistic, meticulous, pedantic, sophistic and joyless. 'Right' or 'wrong' is its usual first response to anybody or anything. Order versus disorder is a core dimension in the mind of the individual, and consistency is highly prized. Absolute certainty is sought, often at the very high price of creativity, which depends on the willingness to risk being mistaken.

Because, as psychoanalysis has pointed out, the obsessive-compulsive personality needs an above-average intelligence quotient to contain its ideational gymnastics, Be Perfect is often the chief personality syndrome of very intelligent people. Some of its most adaptive displacements, and its most constricting limitations are found in the stereotype of the academic.

Typical words used by Be Perfect are: perfect/worthless; clean/dirty; tidy/untidy; should/shouldn't; obviously; as it were; believe; of course; depression; exactly; actually; precisely; It's not my fault; ...for my sins; to me, personally. Be Perfect's tone of voice is measured, accusatory and didactic; facial expression is stern, severe and flushed; posture is robot-like, rigid, stiff and superior. Verbal and body attitudes include: precision; over-qualification; meticulousness, fastidiousness; refusal to be interrupted; itemizing and numbering of points while talking; pursing of bottom lip between forefinger and thumb; clearing throat; punctuating with finger and hand.

Be Perfect's deadly sin is Wrath, against God. Its core defensive aim is the reduction of anxiety by behaving in so blameless a way that Providence is not tempted. Guilt, apprehensive worry, deep disappointment, and depression are favourite negative feelings associated with an existential position of 'I am a worthless sinner.' Most extremely, it is psychotic depression. Projected, it resorts to wrathful shaming of others and, in extreme cases, 'stalking' and murderous aggression. In game-playing, its favourite role is that of Persecutor.

Be Perfect *saves and makes time and money*. At its best, it is the most honourable, constructive, healthy way to live. It is legitimised in organisation, academicism, and religious observance. Its ultimate redemption is in rising above its hubristic attempt to be so in control – ultimately of God! – that death is averted forever. Instead, at its most evolved, it lives life as if it has meaning, even if it doesn't, while at the same time laughingly knowing we may just be God's absurd joke.

Hurry Up is the defence against the fear of life. Its premise is that the universe is essentially malevolent and that life is to be endured painfully until relieved by death. There is no meaning to life and everything is futile.

Nothing is satisfying from the Hurry Up point of view, although it is willing to stay alive while it has the energy to go on looking for the timeless and unconditional love of another human being that it believes would negate the pain of life. This quest is defeated repeatedly, and suspicion and mistrust of people is accumulated in these defeats.

As a personality type, Hurry Up is a close relative of the paranoid syndrome. Moderate degrees of Hurry Up are extremely easy to induce in children in even the most loving families. A child separated, even briefly, from its mother under an age when the meaning of the separation is clearly explicable to his or her Adult, will experience a sense of abandonment, the consequence of which will be a degree of Hurry up in the child's personality. Typically, the child is called on to obey Mother or Father instantly; either she complies and forgoes thinking for herself or she refuses to jump to it and finds that when she does arrive nobody has waited for her and she is left out of things and feels she does not belong. The general atmosphere in such families is tense. Members of the family bicker and screech and shout at each other and rush around frenetically. Things are generally disorganised and chaotic and, from the child's point of view, frighteningly unpredictable. Nobody has time to give the child many strokes at all, and those she does get are usually angry negative ones. The child is treated by the parents as an object that gets tripped over. As often as possible they get the child out of the way, so they don't have to notice him or her at all.

Overall, Hurry Up is manifestly chronically fearful and anxious, in a hurry, jittery, demanding, restless, shifty, manic, late and generally unreliable and ungrateful. Core existential dimensions are: life and misery or death and peace; belonging or not belonging, which is often expressed as a childhood fantasy of having been adopted and really belonging to other, good parents; demand or withdraw; space and aloneness or claustrophobia and people. Hurry Up people are unable to be alone contentedly and yet, when they are with people, they give the impression that they would rather be somewhere else or with somebody else. They are unable to sit still, they tap their fingers and feet impatiently, frown uncomprehendingly at the person talking to them, often giving the impression to the person that he or she has said something offensive.

Typical words used by Hurry Up are: hurry up! time; panic; anxiety; quickly, energy; tired; crazy; it's pointless; it's futile. Hurry Up says 'I' but never 'we'. Her tone of voice is agitated, demanding, staccato; facial expression is blank or frowningly non-comprehending, with brows knitted into vertical lines between the eyes. She speaks rapidly and interrupts herself and others, is breathless and fidgety, impatient, often drinks too much alcohol or takes drugs and drives dangerously.

Hurry Up's deadly sin is Greed. It asks for everything and ends up with nothing. Its core defensive aim is to justify continued existence by frenetically looking for the one person who will love it unconditionally and forever. Favourite bad feelings are fear, panic or terror, which is projected as Let me be your baby. The achieved existential position is, 'I am an outsider. Life is futile.' Most extremely, Hurry Up is manifest as paranoid schizophrenia or mania in which thought processes are so disrupted that meaningful communication with others is broken and inadequate. In game-playing, its favourite role is that of Victim.

Hurry Up *kills time and loses money*. At its best, it is the most spirited, charming and adventurous attitude to life. It is legitimised in occupations involving speed, movement, and risk-taking. Its redemption lies in its coming to terms with the reality that unconditional and timeless positive strokes are not on offer in the world at large, but that conditional strokes are well worth having. Then Hurry Up can be a role model for the refreshing, adventurous spontaneity that spits in the eye of death and makes life worth living.

Please is the defence against the fear of responsibility. It is the response of the child to winning the Oedipal battle, that is, of having been more loved by the opposite-sexed parent than that parent loved the same-sexed parent. It is the 'spoiled brat' syndrome, which consists of a presumption of its entitlement to anything it wants from another. Along with this presumption goes a mixture of guilt and resentment towards the same-sexed parent: guilt for the illegitimacy of her victory over that parent and resentment towards that parent for lacking the power legitimately to defeat the child. Please recapitulates this theme in all its relationships by manipulatively getting what it wants and denying responsibility for having 'done' anything. When it is found out and confronted by another's wrath, it smiles abashedly. This smile represents both its triumph of revenge against its parents, who have so stunted its emotional growth, and a seductive bid to be forgiven on account of its child-like charm.

As a personality type, Please is a close relative of the psycho-analytic passive-aggressive syndrome. Please presumes to read other people's minds and considers having its own mind read to be a positive stroke. Because it doesn't know what it wants, it is glad to have other people tell it what it wants, but when it is called on to express its own wants or feelings it usually utters some platitude or cliché. Please finds its compensation in being relieved of responsibility; if things go wrong, it is the other person's fault. It is so over-adapted that it is virtually cut off from its Free Child. It has been conditioned to believe that all feelings are made to order, and accepts its own obligation only to have 'nice' feelings and to behave in accordance with propriety.

Overall, Please is manifestly 'nice' (and 'nasty'), conventional, respectable, well-mannered, emotionally manipulative, compliant (and defiant), and a busybody. Control or be-controlled is a core dimension. It won't say 'no' to any request, but often manages to forget that it ever said 'yes'. It secretly resents any demands made of it and collects and stores resentment inside itself until, like a balloon, one more puff causes it to burst. The nearest innocent bystander may receive the full force of its explosive accusation that it is being treated like a doormat.

Typical words used by Please are: dear; really? nice; pleasant; y'know; kinda; sorta; I mean...; Please says 'we' rather than 'I' to avoid autonomy and responsibility. Paradoxically, beginning a request with 'please' is a sign of not being in Please, since it forces the user actually to state his or her wishes, and implies the freedom of the other person to respond positively or negatively. Please's tone of voice is pleading, whining, dictating, questioning and patronising; its face is usually averted from directly looking at another person, its eyebrows are often permanently raised, resulting in deep horizontal lines on the forehead; posture is humble and round-shouldered. Verbal and body attitudes include: nodding the head repeatedly while another person is speaking, running fingers through or patting hair, checking appearance in a mirror.

Please's deadly sin is Falsehood. Its core defensive aim is to be good enough to avoid being devoured or abandoned. If a defining characteristic of all the Adapted Child types is inauthenticity, Please is inauthenticity squared. Its favourite bad feeling is embarrassment, which it projects as sulky withdrawal and 'Please yourself!' or a resentful, 'That's not nice'. The strain of 'niceness' inevitably reaches its limit in its episodic outbursts of rudeness and lack of consideration for others, justified as being sick of being put upon. It confirms the existential position of 'Nobody ever gives me what I want' or 'People treat me as if I am bad, but really I am good.' Most extremely, when its feelings are thoroughly repressed, it becomes classical hysteria with conversion symptoms. In game-playing it adroitly weaves its way through each of Persecutor, Rescuer and Victim.

Please *fritters time and money*. At its best, it is the most civilised attitude to life. It is legitimised in hierarchical organisations in which people are bosses and bossed, and in occupations in which a uniform is de rigueur. Its redemption resides in getting in touch with its Free Child, especially acknowledging its 'bad' feelings and being willing to be responsible (and sometimes guilty) for the emotional responses it invokes in others. Then it can be a role model for others as the kindest, most considerate and civilised way to live.

Try Hard is the defence against the fear of failure. It defines the world's losers, and the words 'try' or 'try hard' very reliably imply that whatever it is the individual is setting out to do, he will fail. It is the response of the child having lost the Oedipal battle in a wrong way, namely by the excessive aggression (or, sometimes, the absence or total ineffectualness) of the same-sexed parent. The consequence in the child is an absence of self-esteem, for which he feels humiliated and full of anger. He hovers between the contrary impulses of impotent passivity and rageful pugnacity. He believes that if he fought back against his same-sexed parent he would either be defeated again and even more humiliated; or, if victorious, he would feel himself to be the murderer of his same-sexed parent. His 'trying' is carefully calculated to achieve neither of these fearful outcomes; he uses an enormous amount of energy as if treading water to avoid drowning, but also getting nowhere. Procrastination is a favourite device. His pose may be humble or arrogant, or alternating, but whichever side of the coin is his chosen mask, the other side will be very evident to any sensitive observer. His own and others' aggression cause him a lot of trouble.

As a personality type, Try Hard is a close relative of Adler's 'inferiority complex'. It is resentfully competitive, always putting all his eggs in one grandiose basket, forever being about to make the big time in whatever realm his essential need to fail is focused. Or else he cops out of all competition with rationalisations such as 'I could be the greatest if I could be bothered.' He is a great believer in luck; others get the good sort, while he gets the bad.

Overall, Try Hard is competitive, angry, aggressive, humble, helpless, grandiose, conceited, bitter, militant and sarcastically discounting of others. The Try Hard person starts a dozen projects and finishes none of them. Try Hard seeks out the company of people who are even more Try Hard than itself so that it can look down on them; although it is also eager to be a hanger-on of some other people whom it looks up to. What Try

Hard cannot cope with is the essential reality that we are all better than most other people at a few things, not as good as most people at a few things and equal with every other human being in nearly every respect. Try Hard wants all or nothing and so gets nothing.

Typical words used by Try Hard are: Can you...? could/couldn't; impossible; superior/inferior; fail/succeed; I don't know; it's hard; lucky/unlucky; I'm better than/not as good as you/him/her. Try Hard's tone of voice is angry and sarcastic; its facial expression is puzzled, irritated and worried, often with deep, vertical frown marks between the eyes. Verbal and body attitudes include sitting forward, elbows on knees, chin in hand; asking more than one question at a time; not answering the questions asked; a stuttering impatient manner and clenched fists.

Try Hard's deadly sins are Envy and Sloth. Try Hard is usually manifest as conceit or bitterness. It avoids Heaven and Hell, but lives in Purgatory. The final existential position is, 'I'm a failure' or 'I'm not as good as I think I am.' Most extremely, it becomes pathological narcissism and/or schizoid grandiosity. In game-playing, it alternates between the roles of Persecutor and Victim.

Try Hard *squanders time and money.* At its best, it is diligent, patient, and persistent in working towards its goals. It is legit-imised in occupations requiring patient repetition and where servility and some authorised aggression are combined, such as in the army or police force. Its redemption resides in stopping making excuses for its parents' failures and bitterness, and likewise stopping making excuses for itself; instead, it can then achieve its own healthy self-esteem, without envy or admiration of others, but as equal to equal. Then it can be a role model for modest and contented satisfaction with itself and with life.

Be Strong is the defence against the fear of rejection. It is the

Oedipal response of the child to feeling redundant to the self-sufficient, closed, symbiotic relationship between her parents, irrespective of whether the relationship between the parents was essentially happy or unhappy. Typically, one or other of the parents is so narcissistically embroiled in his or her own Child needs, and the other parent so busy coping with the narcissistic parent's demands, that neither parent has energy left over for giving to the Child of the child. The consequence is that the child neither identifies with her same-sexed parent, nor feels appreciated by her opposite-sexed parent. Consequently, Be Strong children believe they lack the characteristics that are needed to be loveworthy, and they respond with lonely self-sufficiency. Be Strong wears a mask of aloofness and invulnerability to others, which prevents others making intimate contact and so avoids being rejected. 'I don't need or want anybody' is the lie it tells itself and others.

As a personality type, Be Strong is a close relative of autism. It longs for closeness, but in its belief that it is essentially unloveworthy, it decides that it must do without intimacy altogether or be satisfied with a relationship with a very needy other, whose neediness will bind that other to her. She makes a virtue out of what she perceives as a necessity to be solely dependent on herself for strokes to her Child. She is only able to accept a few strokes for her responsible Parent and her sensible Adult.

Overall, Be Strong is manifestly cold, aloof, self-contained, uninvolved, invulnerable, unemotional, independent and a loner. Be Strong talks about feelings, but never shows them. 'Strength' versus 'weakness' is a core dimension; self-discipline is displayed and respected in oneself and others, while mawkishness or any form of wearing one's heart on one's sleeve is deplored. Duty is pleasure. People who express their emotions are judged boring.

Typical words and phrases used by Be Strong are: strong/weak; boring; pull yourself together; I don't care; no comment; vulnerable; duty; childish; it's no good getting upset/crying over spilt milk; you don't appreciate what I'm saying; I feel that ...; that makes me feel...; Be Strong says 'you' or, even more Be Strong, 'one' instead of 'I'. Be Strong's tone of voice is monotonic and dispassionate; its face is moulded, cold, hard, expressionless; posture is erect, rigid and frozen. Verbal and body attitudes include an over-straight back; legs crossed, apparently being totally in Adult, having, if male, a moustache (to hide his upper lip, should it inadvertently slacken), pulling up socks, excessive appreciation for anything given.

Be Strong's deadly sin is Pride. Its core defensive aim is to avoid rejection by not asking for anything. He asks for nothing and so gets nothing. The end result is the recapitulation of the existential position of 'I am unappreciated and unlovable.' Most extremely, it is manifest as isolated autism. In game-playing, its favourite role is that of Rescuer.

Be Strong *uses time and money*. At its best, it is self-sacrificing, generous, brave and utterly reliable. It is legitimised in public service and in occupations that are on the receiving end of people's complaints. Its redemption resides in its willingness to suffer the pain of rejection sometimes in order to succeed, in due course, in receiving (as well as giving) love. Then it can be a role model for others in its courageous stalwartness and dependability in the face of all life's vicissitudes.

Compound Personality Types

By and large, every personality contains characteristics of each of the five types. Together, Be Perfect, Hurry Up, Please, Try Hard, and Be Strong are major components of everybody's Adapted Child, and the Adapted Child is involved in nearly everything we feel, think and do in the course of our waking lives. But these elements are mixed and matched in a large variety of ways in individual human beings. Some people have one element dominatingly present in most of their everyday transactions, while others seem to make use of all five elements in quick succession.

However, over the years when I was developing my understanding of the five basic personality types I noticed that most people seem to have two of the types phenomenally dominant in their personalities. Reflecting on this led me to realise that, for any individual, a particular pair form a significant *compound of duality* in that person's consciousness. (See 'Duality Rules, OK') That is, each of the basic types has some quality *in common* with each of the other types; and, at the same time, each of the basic types has some quality *in conflict* with each of the other types. So for any pair of types there is an element of conflict *and* the resource for reconciling that conflict.

Thus, the basic types are the atoms of personality and the compound types are the molecules; and it is the molecules that represent the basic structure of any individual's consciousness, which can often be easily observed in a person's speech and body language. The ten possible pairings of the five basic types describe ten common personality sub-types.

In this essay I will outline the nature of each of the pairs, their inherent conflicts, and their means of resolving their conflicts into the incipient talents they represent. While the isotopic manifestations of thought, feeling and behaviour of the singular types are manifold, their essentially elementary nature makes a fairly comprehensive account of each of them possible. Insofar as the compounds are manifestations of the enormous overall complexity of any particular personality, any description is bound to be a caricature of any human being it describes. Nevertheless, the stereotypes described by the molecules of the pairs made out of the five atoms can be enormously useful means of inferring, from even the briefest transactions we may have with a stranger on a bus, the core existential positions of people we encounter.

The vignettes that follow are outlines of the usual attributes contained in each of the simplest compounds of personality, including the usual childhood background associated with it, the core existential dichotomy of the compound, the defensive armour associated with it, and the typical existential decision being served.

Be Perfect/Hurry Up. This is the *uncommitted doubter,* who holds in balance the most basic duality in us all, the fear of death and the quest for excitement. *Anxiety* is the commonality of the two components.

In childhood, this personality suffered pain in relation to her parents but was unable to decide whether the fault was in herself or them. The grown-up personality represents a protracted struggle to resolve this uncertainty in which she causes pain to both herself and her parents (so that whichever party is guilty is punished). Outwardly, she may seem very well-balanced, but a great deal of her energy is consumed in maintaining the tenuous balance of her uncertainty.

Manic-depression and alcoholism and drug-addiction are diseases of this personality. Some normal signs are observable in individuals who alternate between thinking too long and too hard, and rashly rushing into things; or who are reliably unreliable to a precise degree, such as always being seven minutes late for appointments; or who want to belong and not belong at the same time, exemplified in people who are members of unusual religious or other communities.

The core dichotomy of this personality is safety or danger (and I once met a man of this type who was profoundly satisfied in his job as a safety officer in a nuclear power plant!). The existential position represented is something like, 'I and the whole world are either mad or bad, but I'm not sure which.' When *uncommitted doubters* transform the guilt in Be Perfect into organisation and the panic in Hurry Up into efficiency, they may become truly *passionate philosophers*.

Be Perfect/Please. This is the *righteous blamer.* The conflict is between absolute and relative standards of morality. Moral control and righteousness are the commonalities of the two components.

Child feelings and Parent beliefs are contaminated in this personality, which declares an incomplete resolution of attachment to the opposite-sexed parent, a common consequence of being spoilt by that parent and having a weak same-sexed parent.

This personality rapidly rises to power in hierarchical organisations, being so capable of both giving and obeying orders and of manipulating other people as well as driving themselves very hard.

The core dichotomy of this personality is control or be controlled and the existential decision it represents is something like, 'If I make the wrong decision I will be culpable and feel guilty, but so long as I make no choice I am being good, so nobody can blame me for what goes wrong.' When *righteous blamers* transform the guilt in Be Perfect into organisation and the feeling of being misunderstood in Please into flexibility they may become truly *responsible leaders*.

Be Perfect/Try Hard. This is the *fighter of lost causes.* The conflict is between absolute and relative achievement. Intellectual rightness is the commonality of the two components.

This personality declares unresolved rivalry with the same-sexed parent, towards whom the child felt timidly inferior and angry.

The grown-up personality is competitive and dominating but also easily humiliated. It is found in occupations like music or sport where there is always room for improvement and success demands constant practice.

The core dichotomy of this personality is victory or defeat, and the existential decision it represents is something like, 'Nobody lives up to my ideals and I'm not as good as I should be either. If I do bad things other people may excuse me, and then I am relieved, but I would feel more loved if they punished me and told me what I've done wrong.' When *fighters of lost causes* transform the guilt in Be Perfect into organisation and the fear of failure in Try Hard into persistence they may become truly *committed champions.*

Be Perfect/Be Strong. This is the *cold intellectual.* The conflict is between emotional intensity and detachment. Rationality is the commonality of the two components.

In childhood, this personality felt redundant in the face of the symbiosis (loving or hateful) between her parents and struggled to feel worthy of being loved.

The grown-up personality demands the right to do things its own way, so they are unlikely to be successful employees unless given lots of autonomy, and are best suited to self-employment. Their emotional vulnerability prompts them to remain aloofly self-sufficient as far as is humanly possible.

The core dichotomy of this personality is self-denial or being rejected, and the existential decision it represents is something like, 'Other people cannot cope with my needs as well as their own. Since their needs are greater than mine I have no right to ask for anything from them. So long as I need nothing from others I will not be tempted to ask for anything, so I can remain blameless.' When *cold intellectuals* transform the guilt in Be Perfect into organisation and the feeling of being unappreciated in Be Strong into resilience they may become truly *independent thinkers.*

Hurry Up/Please. This is the *sorry sinner.* The conflict is between social maladaptiveness and social adaptiveness. Nervous insecurity is the commonality of the components.

In childhood, this personality responded to parental demands by oscillating between 'naughtiness' and apologetic 'niceness'.

The grown-up personality is sparklingly attractive but unreliable. They begin relationships quickly and enthusiastically but can destroy them equally quickly through their hysterical and violent demandingness. They are volatilely unpredictable and both paranoically hostile and symbiotically clinging.

The core dichotomy of this personality is terrifying aloneness or suffocating conformity, and the existential decision it represents is something like, 'I could love life if only I could find somebody to love me in the way I want to be loved, that is, with unconditional love from their Parent to my Child. I try so hard to be good, and sometimes I think I am loved, but then the other person always soon stops loving me and tells me to go to hell.' When *sorry sinners* transform the panic in Hurry Up into efficiency and the feeling of being misunderstood in Please into flexibility they may become truly *lively conformists.*

Hurry Up/Try Hard. This is the *angry outsider.* The conflict is between futility and struggle. Anger is the commonality of the components.

The childhood experience of this personality often includes being subject to abusive violence.

The grown-up personality balances feeling an inferior failure with being an alienated outsider. In extremis, it is Hell's Angels and violent criminals. Less extremely, they are con men, militant trade-unionists, militant women's rights advocates ...or militant anything. The passive version is the derelict or laid back drop-out. In general, they are snarling, derisive and cynical. They hate 'the system' and all authority figures, and only work at all for the money they need for their personal, usually profligate, pleasures.

The core dichotomy of this personality is rage or futility, and the existential decision it represents is something like, 'There's nothing you can do for me or give me and I'll punch you if you try. I'm no good but neither are you. The world is one big shit heap.' When *angry outsiders* transform the panic in Hurry Up into efficiency and the fear of failure in Try Hard into persistence they may become truly *roving adventurers*.

Hurry Up/Be Strong. This is the *frightened loner*. The conflict is between terrified neediness and aloof self-sufficiency. Fear and coldness are the commonalities of the components.

The childhood experience of this personality is one of extreme stroke-deprivation, possibly including abandonment.

The grown-up personality is the most isolated of the types. It is very vulnerable to all kinds of self-destructive behaviour. Positively, they are courageous adventurers and heroes, such as solo yachtsmen, polar explorers and mountaineers. Women with this personality are often made briefly happy in becoming mothers, whereby they are able to perceive the utter dependency of their infants as an expression of unconditional love given them by their infants to them.

The core dichotomy of this personality is reject or be rejected and the existential decision it represents is something like, 'I can make no sense of people or the world. The world is strange and cold and I am lost in it. Anyone who loves me is a shit.' When *frightened loners* transform the panic in Hurry Up into efficiency and the feeling of being unappreciated in Be Strong into resilience they may become truly *brave individualists*.

Please/Try Hard. This is the *humble servant*. The conflict is between niceness and nastiness. Lack of autonomy is the commonality of the components.

The childhood experience of this personality is of the demand to be 'nice' to the opposite-sexed parent and unchallengingly respectful and obedient to the same-sexed parent.

The grown-up personality struggles to balance conformity and self-esteem. It is stereotypically working class and respectable. It is timid, proper, conventional, knows its place and does not question life as it finds it. But it is not without pride, and it can be patronising as well as servile. It is usually content to stay in lowly occupations that offer long-term security, which it values above expectations of promotion and increased earnings. It gains self-esteem through association with its employer's status.

The core dichotomy of this personality is niceness or power, and the existential decision is something like, 'As long as people do as they are told no harm will come to them.' When *humble servants* transform the feeling of being misunderstood in Please into flexibility and the fear of failure in Try Hard into persistence they may become truly *contented workers*.

Please/Be Strong. This is the *do-gooder*. The conflict is between compliance and autonomy. Do-gooding is the commonality of the components.

The childhood experience of this personality is the demand for propriety and consideration of others' feelings above her own.

The grown-up personality is courteous, considerate, nice but sometimes nasty; practical and helpful but also aloof, uptight, and secretly resentful of the impositions of others on their goodwill. It is the personality type most associated with the helping professions, like nursing, voluntary aid, social work and any occupations where pleasant responsiveness to others' needs or demands is called for. Do-gooders doubt their own loveworthiness and find it difficult to accept strokes for just being themselves; but they can more readily accept strokes if they feel they have earned them through unselfish giving to others.

The core dichotomy of this compound is control or vulnerability, and the existential decision it represents is something like, 'I look after others when, by rights, they should be looking after me.' When *do-gooders* transform the feeling of being misunderstood in Please into flexibility and the feeling of being unappreciated in Be Strong into resilience they may become truly *generous carers*.

Try Hard/Be Strong. This is the *proud loser.* The conflict is between crippled humiliation and resilient strength. Resentment is the commonality of the components.

The childhood experience of this personality is of his parents' bitter resentment about 'their lot'.

The grown-up personality balances feeling inferior with aloof non-competitiveness. It is often exploited by others because, although they may have much to offer, their self-conscious timidity prevents them declaring their ideas soon enough to be heard. So more self-confident rivals may steal their good ideas and get credit for them. They typically dislike but endure their work, whatever it is. Because they are so little noticed in their jobs they tend to withdraw into their private dreams.

The core dichotomy of this personality is frustration or resignation, and the existential decision it represents is something like, 'The struggle to get what I want is not worthwhile because successful people never appreciate my worth, so I'd rather be with losers who I know are inferior to me.' When *proud losers* transform the fear of failure in Try Hard into persistence and the feeling unappreciated in Be Strong into resilience they may become truly *quiet achievers.*

Cultures, like individuals, have personalities. So, too, do domes-ticated animals, and pets are obviously chosen for the compati-bility – by identification or complementarity – between them and their owners.

Climate is an influence on a nation's personality. The cold climates of northern Europe tend to induce Be Strong, the warmer climates of middle Europe tend to Please, and the very hot climates of southern Europe tend to Hurry Up. And any culture in which religion is a powerful background force is inevitably Be Perfect.

I propose – mostly for fun – the following national stereo-types: the English are Be Strong/Please. The Irish are Be Perfect/Hurry Up (Hurry Up tending to dominate). The Welsh are Try Hard/Be Strong (especially about their language). The Scots are Be Perfect/Be Strong. The French are overwhelmingly Be Perfect (focused on food, sex, and the purity and pronunci-ation of their language). The Germans are Be Perfect/Please (to be successful and respected). The Italians are Be Perfect/Hurry Up (Be Perfect dominating in the aesthetic aspects of life, Hurry Up in government). The Americans are Hurry Up/Try Hard (to be loved and make a billion dollars). The Israelis are Be Perfect/Please (to be righteous in their own and others' estimation). The Arab nations are Be Perfect/Try Hard (to get revenge). Northern European countries tend, like the English to be Please/Be Strong. Eastern Europeans tend to Be Perfect/Try Hard. The Australians are Hurry Up/Try Hard (to have a good time and be culturally respected). The Japanese are Please/Try Hard (to be nice and rigidly to persist).

Cats are Be Strong, dogs are Please, horses are Hurry Up.

Personality Types in Relationships

The two most fascinating considerations concerning people are the samenesses and the differences between them. We are all alike and all different. Compatibility and incompatibility may be observed in samenesses between any two people; and compatibility and incompatibility may be observed in differences between any two people.

We are all alike in wanting strokes from others and in seeking repeated validation of the profound, largely unconscious, existential decisions we formulated in early childhood. We are all different in the particularity of the strokes we seek and the particularity of the existential decisions we seek continuously to validate by reaffirmation.

The first requirement for us to function effectively in any transaction with any other human being is a minimum knowledge of 'human nature', through which we recognise the commonality of all people everywhere in their general needs and frailties. People who interact with others with an implicit consciousness of the primary samenesses rather than the differences between all people exude a modest warmth that never fails to attract people to them. In my opinion, this is the *sine qua non* of all lovingness; but it is not sufficient for intimacy.

Without any knowledge of the differences between ourselves and any other, our essential narcissism impels us to treat the other as if he or she were identical with ourselves; so whether or not we please him or her is bound to be fortuitous. 'Good manners' facilitate us in pleasing all people at a minimum superficial level, at least within the bounds of the culture to which our particular 'good manners' apply; but to achieve any degree of intimacy with another, some acquired knowledge of our own and the other's idiosyncratic natures is needed.

At a purely biological, Natural Child, level, the discriminations we make between people are very crude. Like other animals, our essential narcissism usually dictates that we prefer others who reflect back to us our own image, mostly in terms of colouring, shape and size. We are all probably also attracted to general robustness and other characteristics associated with the survival of the fittest.

But the turn-ons that excite us most – the psychological parts of our responses to others that overlay our basic animal nature – are all informed by our Adapted Child. Simple, physical orgasm is not a patch on 'the real thing', which is, uniquely for human beings, a physical response compounded with emotionality and consists of a huge variety of possibilities that Freud subsumed in the general dichotomy of sadism and masochism. There are pleasures in our pains and pains in our pleasures, and the compulsive nature of our Adapted Child testifies to this truth.

Like it or not, we fall in love with a chosen other for the immediate, albeit usually unconscious, knowledge we have that that other, in his or her way of being, will willingly co-operate with us in confirming the validity of our childhood decisions concerning the pains as well as the joys that will be our lot in life. And notwithstanding the superficial and facile observations and judgements people may make about any couple, all intimate relationships are, by definition, between equals. We are never truly misled. In every 'bad' that is done us by our intimate partners, we have colluded. A needed person has as much need to be needed as a needy one needs; a Victim has as much desire to be Victimised as a Rescuer or Persecutor has to Rescue or Persecute. In every touch between one person and another that binds them, the touching surfaces, by definition, adhere equally to each other. If and when this equality no longer applies, a couple becomes unstuck and parts; as long as they are together they are equal in their attachment, whether the attachment be essentially based on loving joy, the agonies of purgatory or hell, or something in-between.

There are fifteen possible relationships between the Adapted Child of one person and the Adapted Child of another: five relationships between like types and ten relationships between different types. Since most people have two types at the core of their personalities, the Adapted Child to Adapted Child relationship of any two people is typically made up of four discrete ways of relating, each of which has its own discrete pleasures and pains. For example, if one person's Adapted Child is, at core, Be Perfect and Hurry Up, and another's Be Perfect and Please, there will be a Be Perfect to Be Perfect aspect to their relationship, a Be Perfect to Please aspect, a Hurry Up to Be Perfect aspect, and a Hurry Up to Please aspect; and the couple will experience these aspects as very distinct parts of their relationship. Given that there is no escaping the predominance of our Adapted Childs in our relationships, it can be very useful to a couple to analyse the Adapted Child to Adapted Child part of their relationship into its separate components. By this means the couples are able self-consciously to prefer the pleasanter aspects of their relationship and avoid the nastier aspects, while still realistically acknowledging the inevitable centrality of Adapted Child to Adapted Child transactions in their total relationship.

Out of many years' experience, my diagnoses of the fifteen possible couplings between the five personality types can be taken as very reliable, although the descriptions are inevitably exaggerated stereotypes when applied to the realities of a particular relationship. In the vignettes that follow it is merely my intention to communicate the general flavour of what to expect from each of the pairings; the usefulness of my descriptions will depend on the reader's willingness to translate my comments imaginatively into the realm of his or her own experience. Nevertheless, I hope that my comments reflect sufficiently commonplace experience that the reader will, in many cases, readily match his or her own observations to mine. (Where I designate one of a pair as 'he' and the other as 'she' I do so for the sake of verbal simplicity. Men and women are intrinsically equally able to adopt either role in all of the possible pairings.)

Be Perfect and Be Perfect. Like most couplings of like-to-like, this pair usually get on well with each other. They are apt to be united in their common beliefs and values, and so long as they do not disagree fundamentally about what is and is not important in life, they give each other the security of feeling right about things. Their life together tends to be ritualistic, extremely well organised and ordered. Responsibilities are clearly articulated and divided between them, which they each fulfil dutifully and meticulously. Ideally, they tease each other out of excessive rigidity and intolerance. However, if they do disagree fundamentally about their values, they will bicker and criticise each other interminably and probably end up feeling intransigent mutual hatred. A negative Be Perfect to Be Perfect relationship is epitomised in the internecine war in Northern Ireland, the Israel-Arab conflict, and in all religious wars that have ever been fought.

In working relationships this pair is good in an equal relationship or if the subordinate fully respects the boss.

Be Perfect and Hurry Up. At the profoundest levels of their personalities this couple is supremely well-matched because they are respectively the expressions of the fear of death and the temptation of death. To this extent, Be Perfectly is a cowardly stick-in-the-mud and Hurry Up is a brazen daredevil. They are able to cancel out the unhealthy extreme that each on its own stands for and to create instead an optimally healthy balance between organisation and efficiency, thrift and extravagance, caution and daring, structure and spontaneity, right-wing and left-wing politics ... and many other adaptive compromises between a wide range of polarities in life. Transactionally, Be

Perfect tends to play the role of sometimes indulgent and sometimes controlling Parent to the sometimes charming and sometimes exasperating Child of Hurry Up. Only if they escalate their natures to a pathological degree can they harm each other by colliding in murderous/suicidal insanity.

This can be an enjoyably volatile pairing in a working relationship if Be Perfect is the boss; if Hurry Up is the boss, it only works if Be Perfect is given lots of autonomy.

Be Perfect and Please. This relationship is usually stable and contented, based on agreed dominance and submission roles. Be Perfect is the boss and Please is happily obedient. Be Perfect's quest for having things exactly the way he wants is fulfilled and Please is profoundly reassured in knowing she is doing the right and good thing. 'You have done well,' given by Be Perfect is usually received by Please as a positive stroke even though others might resent the patronage implied. However, because of their contented equilibrium, Be Perfect tends to lack any challenge to his rigidity and Please is not stretched to live outside her repressive conventionality. Sometimes, Please episodically expresses some defiant rebelliousness and Be Perfect responds with angry criticism. But Be Perfect controls the outburst of Please and things usually return rapidly to their normal peace and calm.

In working relationships, this is a very good coupling if Be Perfect is the boss; a bad coupling if Please is the boss.

Be Perfect and Try Hard. This relationship is an obviously unhappy one, based on open warfare. Each is critical of the other, but Be Perfect, who tends to be the more intelligent in this partnership, is the one who is consistently the victorious Persecutor while Try Hard is the humiliated Victim. Try Hard admires and envies Be Perfect's conviction of her rightness, and Be Perfect disdains Try Hard. Be Perfect is using Try Hard to project her own feeling of worthlessness onto another, while Try Hard is reinforced in his fundamental belief that 'No matter how hard I try, I'll never be successful enough.' Be Perfect often threatens to leave Try Hard but she secretly knows that she is dependent on Try Hard for her needed feeling of superiority. Both know their relationship is likely to continue in its often violent unhappiness for a long time.

In working relationships, this pairing is very humiliating for Try Hard if Be Perfect is the boss; it is a short-lived relationship if Try Hard is the boss.

Be Perfect and Be Strong. This couple is united by a puritanical attitude to life. They are both ambitious and work hard to achieve their goals. Be Perfect easily accommodates to Be Strong's view that reliability is the better part of love, and Be Strong pleases Be Perfect by being willing to get on with things dutifully without complaining. They are likely to enjoy conversations with each other that are serious, playfully critical, and ironical. They are unlikely to cause each other much pain although they tend to reinforce rather than modify each other's essential over-conscientiousness at the expense of Free Child spontaneity and pleasure. In their bossy righteousness they are very similar although Be Perfect is passionate where Be Strong is cool. To this extent, Be Perfect may accuse Be Strong of being cold and Be Strong may accuse Be Perfect of being prejudicially overly involved.

In working relationships, this is generally a good 'get-on-with-it' partnership.

Hurry Up and Hurry Up. Since the deep – however unconscious – intention of Hurry Up in relation to others is, 'I'll reject you before you can reject me,' an intimate relationship between two people who are both principally Hurry Up is so unstable that it is unlikely to be formed at all. Phenomenally, though, each is obsessed with finding unconditional and lasting love. So when two Hurry Ups meet they often experience themselves as falling passionately in love at first sight, and tend to fall straight into bed with each other at their first meeting. The relationship usually ends a short time later when one of them simply doesn't turn up to an arranged meeting or in some way expresses as much hateful lack of regard for the other as he or she expressed loving commitment at their first meeting. As casual friends, they will tend to get drunk or 'stoned out of their minds' together.

They are unlikely to form a working relationship of any duration.

Hurry Up and Please. For Hurry Up, his relationship with Please is nearly as good as a relationship with Be Perfect. Although Be Perfect offers more of the control that Hurry Up so desperately needs, Please offers Hurry Up considerable reassurance. Hurry Up says, 'It's no good expecting love to last. People give it to you for a little while, then they inevitably abandon you.' To which Please replies, 'I know how you feel, how frightening it is to think of being left alone. But it's not inevitable. So long as you are good the people who love you will stay with you forever. Let me show you how to be good.' Through this implicit dialogue Hurry Up learns social adaptiveness and his terror is diminished; and Please gains the reassurance of security she gets from knowing her partner's emotional dependence on their relationship is even greater than her own.

In working relationships, this couple like each other.

Hurry Up and Try Hard. This relationship is full of tension and aggression. Try Hard is driven crazy by Hurry Up, and Hurry Up is made wildly impatient by Try Hard. Hurry Up needs a self-confidently controlling other, but Try Hard can only manage the aggression of *un*self-confidence. And Hurry Up, being completely absorbed in her own neediness, is incapable of giving Try Hard the 'tough love' he needs to overcome his inferiority complex. Each justifies his or her inadequacies in terms of the provocation of the other. Hurry Up says, 'If he weren't so damn slow I could be calm.' Try Hard says, 'If only she'd give me some peace I could fulfil my ambitions and my potential.' Neither of them achieves anything positive by this dishonest projection of responsibility for their hang-ups but they may eventually succeed in provoking violence or serious bodily illness in each other.

In working relationships, this pair are engaged in open warfare.

Hurry Up and Be Strong. This is probably the most painful relationship of all. Each is convinced of the inevitability of profound loneliness, and they powerfully support each other's affirmation of this conviction. The relationship usually begins with Be Strong as Rescuer of Hurry Up as Victim, but Hurry Up quickly begins Persecuting Be Strong who then becomes the Victim. Hurry Up proves that love offered is not enough and doesn't last anyway, and Be Strong proves that what he has to offer is unappreciated; therefore he must be unworthy of love. That these two choose to form a relationship with each other at all bears witness to the sad truth that they are both so unused to receiving love that they would be unable to cope with a relationship that offered it. Hurry Up asks for everything and gets nothing; Be Strong asks for nothing and gets nothing.

In working relationships, this pair are frightened of each other.

Please and Please. This couple is usually united in a stable relationship of mutual dependence. Each of them is terrified of being left alone, so they are both rigidly obedient to their unspoken agreement that they will behave towards each other in accordance with conventional propriety in general and in the ways each other ask in particular. Thus they achieve the emotional security they crave above all else. The price they pay is the stifling of spontaneity and authentic expression of emotion. Neither risks offending the other and so disturbing the safe equilibrium of the relationship, but to an outsider the suppressed resentment between them is often palpable. Sometimes this relationship continues on an even keel for a lifetime; sometimes the essential politeness of the relationship is punctuated with periodic angry quarrels which release the built-up resentment each feels for his or her symbiotic dependence on the other.

In working relationships, this pair empathically identify with each other.

Please and Try Hard. This is likely to be an amicable but dreary relationship. That is, neither is likely to hurt the other, but neither will they stimulate each other to reach beyond the narrowly unambitious and respectable limits they impose on their lives. They 'know their place' and accept it. In England, it is a proto-typical lower-middle-class marriage in which the wife is the Please and the husband the Try Hard partner. Please is nice to Try Hard in not pressing him to achieve anything, and Try Hard validates in his behaviour Please's need to be respectable. The worst they are likely to do to each other from time to time is for Try Hard to think, but rarely say aloud, that Please is affected and pretentious; and for Please to think, but rarely say aloud, that Try Hard is a failure.

In working relationships, this pair are kind to each other.

Please and Be Strong. This relationship is basically an unhappy one, but one which often endures for a lifetime. It is frequently the chief component of English middle-class marriages, the husband being the Be Strong and the wife the Please partner. The trouble is that the relationship offers each of them easy affir-mation of their most painful feelings without providing any positive compensations. Please is dependent on another's instructions as to how to behave to please the other person; Be Strong longs to have his needs understood and met without his having to give voice to them. Please asks Be Strong to tell her what to be and do; Be Strong replies, 'I want you to give to me in a spontaneous and authentic way, not according to instructions.' Thus Please feels misunderstood and falsely vilified; and Be Strong feels unappreciated and unloved.

In working relationships, this pair dislike each other.

Try Hard and Try Hard. Of all the like-to-like relationships between types this is the one least likely to work for the benefit of both partners. (Hurry Up and Hurry Up is equally unbeneficial to both parties but rarely endures for more than a few months anyhow.) At best, Try Hard and Try Hard may be united in hostility and envy towards most other people which may, for example, find expression in their working together for an angry cause. However, more usually, the envious hostility of each is projected onto the intimate other, with each chronically criticising the other in order to boost his or her own very precarious self-esteem. Each tends secretly to sabotage the other's achievement of his or her ambitions, and they are both constantly on tenterhooks lest the other win over them in some way. Life for this couple is one long aggressive competition.

In working relationships, this pair are competitively aggressive towards each other. They may sometimes unite to fight 'authority' together.

Try Hard and Be Strong. These two are basically incompatible types who are essentially incapable of gratifying each other, so a lasting relationship between them is unlikely. Try Hard asks for what she wants materially in such a way as not to achieve it; Be Strong asks for what he wants emotionally in such a way as to not get it. They are on different wavelengths. Try Hard is competitively aggressive toward Be Strong, and Be Strong adopts a stance of cold and bored aloofness towards Try Hard. Try Hard envies Be Strong his cool control, which Try Hard perceives herself as lacking because of insufficient opportunity; and Be Strong finds Try Hard a bore for wearing her heart on her sleeve. In transacting with each other Be Strong generally limits himself to peremptory brush-offs to Try Hard, and Try Hard is consumed with frustration and rage.

In working relationships, there is mutual resentment and misunderstanding between this pair.

Be Strong and Be Strong. This relationship is characterised by a great deal of mutual independence. Each is especially averse to what they would call emotional suffocation, so they support each other's need for regular periods of separateness to pursue private interests or just be alone. They share the conviction that reliability is the better part of love. So long as both have important interests outside as well as within the relationship they get on very well together and are grateful for their intimacy and commitment to each other, which relieves them of the pain they each experienced as single people reaching out for love. If one of them does not have an important interest outside the relationship he or she will become resentful of the lack of time given to the relationship by the other; one will feel neglected and the other harassed.

In working relationships, this pair generally get on very well, in a spirit of mutual confident reliance on each other.

Irrespective of personality types, within the context of our culture it is my observation that an overwhelmingly important determinant of compatibility or incompatibility between a couple are the *degree and kinds of pain* that each of the individuals experienced in his or her childhood. There can be no profound compatibility between somebody who had an essentially happy childhood and somebody who had an essentially miserable one. The more the experienced *quantities* of unhappiness match, the more compatible the couple will be.

For a good marriage, the *kinds of unhappiness* each experienced may be like-to-like or complementary. So, for example, if each was orphaned in early childhood the relationship has the potential for the rare profundity that shared suffering can bring. An example of a complementary relationship would be one where one partner was suffocatingly smother-loved and the other was the oldest of a large family and was never allowed to be a 'real' child.

Complementary relationships are easier than empathic ones. In complementary relationships the partners can immediately fall into their long-practised, familiar roles with each other. Empathic relationships, though, in order to survive, have to face the challenge of developing together those personality characteristics that make for wholeness, which neither of the partners in the beginning possesses. Two playful children soon realise that somebody has to pay the gas bill, and each will demand nurturing Parent from the other when the need arises, and the role of parenting is one they both have to learn. Conversely, two ultra-responsible people have no models in each other on which to base and develop the capacity for irresponsible, joyous expressiveness that they both so need. Nevertheless, if the challenges of a deeply empathic relationship are faced and worked through, the eventual outcome is likely to be a love of rare depth and permanency.

But whether a relationship is essentially empathic or complementary, it is important that there be gender symmetry between the couple in the playing out and working through of the pains they bring with them from childhood. If one partner's significant pains were experienced through his or her opposite-sexed parent, so should the other partner's be. When there is asymmetry in this respect, although degree and kind of pain experienced may make for attraction between the couple, at the deeper levels of their being their 'wires are crossed' and their intimate relationship is likely to be fraught with many non-verbal misunderstandings.

An ideal marriage is probably one where, through well-matched characteristics, each of the individuals is enabled, projectively, through the other, to exorcise the ghosts of his and her parents' marriages. In the realm of intimate relationships the greatest triumph and joy for each of us is found when we *revenge ourselves* on our parents by being *better than* the parent we most blame, and we *make happier* – through displacement onto our chosen mate – our other parent who, we believe, was most sadly deprived. For the individuals who make up a couple, their separate myths may be utterly disparate. All that matters is that each of them is perceived by the other to be *like and different from* their respective parents in just the ways that matter.

As Spinoza put it, 'Love is nothing else but pleasure accompanied by the idea of external cause; hate is nothing else but pain accompanied by the idea of an external cause.'

We are all inventions of each other.

The Enemies of Love

Lovingness, which is based on our positive self-esteem, is the root of all goodness in us; righteousness, which is based on our fears about ourselves, that is, our negative self-esteem, is the root of all evil in us.

In our relationships there is more or less continuous dialogue between the lovingness and righteousness in ourselves and the lovingness and righteousness in the other. When lovingness in ourselves and another predominates over righteousness, love can be made and maintained; when righteousness in ourselves and another predominates over lovingness, love will be killed or is already dead.

Love *is* what makes the world go round, because it is the currency of the most basic contract each human being makes with the rest of the world: I will look after you, even if you can be of no use to me, if you will look after me likewise. The comparative rarity of infanticide and granny-bashing rests wholly on the construct of 'love' which, like finding intrinsic interest in things and people outside ourselves, is taught by precept so early in life as to become second nature. But interest in anything, and love for anybody, can only be expressed with energy that we have *left-over* after our own survival needs are met. The inauthentic righteousness of our Adapted Child represents our specious bid for our self-preservation.

Our inauthentic righteousness is in need of constant reinforcement to maintain the very tenuous belief in our goodness that it gives us. 'I am holier than thou' is the belief we seek to protect ourselves from our fears. This is the antithesis of the equality which is the only medium in which love thrives.

Being loving means willingly making other people feel good about themselves. It is giving thoughtful and genuine positive strokes. The best are Child to Child, which effectively say, 'You make me feel good' – which makes the other person feel good!

Ritual good manners are the devices we are taught for behaving lovingly towards everybody even if we don't love them. There are stimuli that are usually understood to make the giving of a small positive stroke to another mandatory, such as saying please and thank you and excuse me a multitude of times in our mundane transactions.

But the more idiosyncratically pleasing a stroke is to the receiver, the more nourishing it is. So the better we know someone the more loving we can be to him or her. We know people through the answers they give to the questions we ask them. There is nothing more loving than asking questions.

We value and protect our narcissistic concepts of ourselves – intelligent, kind, generous, compassionate, etc. – because these concepts of our self-esteem are the currencies we use in bartering with others to persuade them that we are of use to them and so deserving of them extending consideration to us (as well as to themselves). The positive psychological attributes we believe ourselves to possess are the ways in which we define ourselves as 'good', and therefore deserving of positive strokes from others.

In an ideal world we would all be assuredly confident of the overwhelming 'goodness' of our attributes and thus assuredly confident of our intrinsic loveworthiness. But, of course, we are not assuredly confident of our overwhelming 'goodness' and associated loveworthiness. To a greater or lesser extent, we all have doubts about our own 'goodness', based on the negative strokes we received as children. People have negative as well as positive self-esteem, and attribute to themselves a whole range of 'bad' characteristics – stupidity, incompetence, selfishness, greed, etc. – by which they fear they are unworthy of love.

The bad in us frightens us; we fear that we will be found out and punished.

We *are* good to the extent that we believe we are good; we *are*

bad to the extent that we believe we are bad. The defensive structures of our Adapted Childs are the devices we deploy in our
struggles to turn our 'badness' into 'goodness' and to convince
ourselves that we are *not responsible* for the punishments of our
most painful, reiterated, negative strokes. *Righteousness is the
camouflage for our negative self-esteem.* While none of us is ever free
of fear and its cloak of righteousness, the greater our authentic,
positive self-esteem, the greater our ability to love. Love is the
root of all goodness; fear is the root of all evil. Our fears make us
keep our partners locked in their fears. Fear and its attendant
righteousness is the cancerous enemy of love.

Each of the five basic Adapted Child personality structures
has its own particular form of righteousness.

Duty. 'Duty' is the righteousness component in Be Perfect. It is
the most righteous of all the righteous. It plays the role of
Persecutor. It humiliates and implicitly reduces to zero the value
of the other. It effectively says, 'You are a deep disappointment to
me and are not worthy of love. However, I married you (or
otherwise committed myself to you), so I will not let you down.
You will find me faultless in the fulfilment of my obligations, but
that is all you are entitled to. Loving you is not part of my obligation to you, and I don't love you, because you have failed in your
obligations to me and have killed my love.'

'Duty' holds itself superior to all lesser mortals who 'imper-
fectly' may dissolve their contractual commitments when love
has died. Its guilt, self-hatred and depression are so great that
only supreme righteousness is enough to hold them at bay. 'Duty'
has probably itself been similarly treated in childhood – dutifully
cared for, without tenderness – and has grown up longing for the
tender love it never got. But so idealised is its notion of love that
it is bound to be disappointed. Behind its intimidating, arrogant,
hard facade its experience of life is agonising. *Its terror is of
change*, because it knows that any change, however slight, would

diminish its absolute *control* over itself and its environment, which is its only safeguard against the suicidal risk of its excruciating pain. It knows what love is, and longs to receive and give it, but chooses a partner unable or unwilling to give love. It recapitulates the nightmare of its childhood, with itself now in the role of the autocratic, dominating parent. Its denial of love for the other is the only outlet for the rage which it actually feels towards its own dominating parent.

Only another whose equally high moral standards it respects is capable of enabling 'Duty' to find its redemption in *tenderness* – towards itself and others.

Need. 'Need' is the righteousness component in Hurry Up. It is the least righteous of all the righteous because it is stuck at a pre-Oedipal developmental stage, before the concepts of 'goodness' and 'love' are really known. Its interest in the world and other people is very slight, and it animates people as if they were 'transitional objects' – teddy bears who are not real, but can be fantasized as real according to its own needs, and who retain their comforting sewn-on smiles no matter how much it bashes them. It plays the role of Victim. It effectively says, 'You have *got* to give me everything I want. I am your baby and you are my Mummy/Daddy. In return, I will sometimes be nice to you and play Koochi-koochi-koo (sex) with you. If you don't do everything I want you to do for me, I'll scream and I'll scream and I'll scream ... until you do.'

'Need' is overwhelmed by fear and desperate to be safely contained by another who will relieve it of all responsibilities. It is so unknowing and inept in maintaining its own basic survival that it is utterly self-centred and greedy. 'Need' was powerfully traumatised by some form of abandonment or abuse before the age of three, and has not developed its self-sufficiency beyond that age. *Its terror is of being alone,* because being alone reduces it to the *helplessness* of an abandoned infant. It does not know what

love is, although it will claim it has 'fallen in love' instantaneously with anybody who is willing to take care of it, and it
immediately offers itself sexually in its bid to secure the other's
love. In the sexual embrace it manages, for a moment, to believe
it is unconditionally and timelessly bonded to the other, but the
other's subsequent expression of separate individuality justifies it
in feeling abandoned and desperate, which it expresses as
hatefulness and hostility. It destroys love before it even begins.

Symbiosis is *not* relating. Babies do *not* relate to their mothers;
their smiles and clinging are designed by nature to invoke the
willing fulfilment of their needs by their mothers. The one-way
love of a mother for her baby is the *only* one-sided love that can
be maintained. All other loves are between two fundamentally
separate, self-sufficient individuals who come together in
wonder and desire, making I, Thou, and Us.

Only if and when Need is willing to forgo the repeated
anxious excitement of the chase after its dream of *the one* who will
give it the unconditional, timeless love of a mother to her baby, in
favour of being willing to *look after itself adequately*, will it be
capable of the giving as well as the taking on which the
experience of love depends.

Expediency. 'Expediency' is the righteousness component of
Please. It is supremely manipulative and makes itself unconscious of what it is doing so as to remain 'innocent'. It plays all
three roles of Rescuer, Persecutor and Victim. It effectively says,
'You are more powerful than I am and make me do as you want.
I know you will always win in open battle, but I will get my
revenge on your domination of me by obeying "the letter of your
law" while hurting you in ways you cannot quite put your finger
on. This will be my triumph. I will help you (Rescuer) or be
obedient to you (Victim), but I'll never give you any genuine
feeling. This will hurt you deeply (Persecutor), but you will have
no right to complain because *you won't be able to fault what I do.'*

'Expediency' cannot afford to be fully conscious of what it is doing because it would then be obliged to accept equal responsibility with the other for the pain between them; and in repressing this knowledge it inevitably represses much other knowledge as well. It is replaying with its present partner its incomplete separation from its opposite-sexed parent, on whom it is *resentfully dependent*. Behind its 'niceness', it is a nervous wreck, because *its terror is of the truth*. Emotional depth and complexity are dangers to be avoided at all cost, because they threaten to expose the guilty secret of its *incestuous desires*. 'Expediency' blushes more than any other enemy of love. It wants to live life lazily and comfortably on the 'nice' surface. Its blinkered tunnel vision keeps out the shadows *and* the sunshine of life.

Only through another who has the strength of love for it to force it to *moral responsibility*, by denying it any instructions to which it can be manipulatively 'obedient', can 'Expediency' gain permission to accept and relish the pain and the joy of true intimacy.

Togetherness. 'Togetherness' is the righteousness component in Try Hard. It is extremely aggressive, which gets it into a lot of trouble, so it periodically retreats into pathetic helplessness in a bid for pity rather than the anger it usually invokes in others. It plays the roles of Persecutor and Victim. It effectively says, 'I know I am a failure, but I can't bear to know this. You have to be my ally in blaming the unfairness of the world for my lack of success. If you don't, I'll make you a worse failure than I am and so make myself feel a success by constantly comparing myself to you.'

'Togetherness' hates and envies self-confident others, and looks for and clings to another who is at least as unself-confident as itself, in a bid to ward itself off from the rest of the world through the enclosed self-sufficiency of its symbiosis with its partner. It is replaying with its present partner its incomplete separation from its same-sexed parent, towards whom it feels inferior and impotently angry. *Its terror is of autonomy,* because it would then have to face its cowardice towards honestly competing with others and, consequently, realistically *acknowledging the limits of its own abilities.* Only by experiencing itself as potentially *the* most powerful person can it keep at bay the fear that it may never be as powerful as its same-sexed parent. It oscillates between playing the role of its aggressively humiliating same-sexed parent, and being the frightened, helpless child in its relationship to its partner. It wears itself out in the aggressive role, and is likely to 'mellow' into cynical bitterness and sexual as well as general impotence in its relationship to the world.

Only another who can give it the 'tough love' of pitilessly pushing it relentlessly to work for the fulfilment of its ambitions can 'Togetheness' gain permission to *fulfil its potential and gain sexy self-esteem.*

'Sex'. 'Sex' is the righteous component in Be Strong. It uses sex as a way of righteously avoiding acknowledging its cold unwillingness to be touched by another. It plays the role of Rescuer. It effectively says, 'I know you would reject me if I asked for anything from you, because I am unloveworthy, so I'll never show you my feelings and you'll never be able to hurt me. I'll hold you in my power by your need of me and my knowledge of *your* vulnerabilities, but you'll never catch me saying I love you.'

'Sex' avoids intimacy under the camouflage of 'intimacy'. (As the more salacious Sunday newspapers used to put it, 'Intimacy then took place.') It is reiterating its defence against the pain it felt in childhood in response to its *valuelessness* to its parents. Its parents – happily or unhappily – were self-sufficient in their symbiosis with each other, and the child withdrew, wounded, from its failed bid to have a significant emotional impact on their relationship. *'Sex's terror is of vulnerability,* because it believes vulnerability must inevitably lead to rejection, so it avoids intimacy by choosing a partner who either, like itself, fears vulnerability and so maintains a reciprocal emotional distance, or one who is so 'needy' as to be incapable of true intimacy. 'Sex' pays the price of deep loneliness, its only gratification being the smug, false strokes it gives itself or gets from others for its 'altruistic' self-denial.

Only another who sees through 'Sex's invulnerable facade and is willing, very gently and repeatedly, to affirm its loveworthiness, can 'Sex' be enabled to gain permission to reveal its wounded heart and be rewarded with the ecstasy of the experience of *sex as the expression of emotional involvement*, rather than the 'enjoyable' mechanical satisfaction of a physiological need, which is all 'Sex' knows.

Men and Women

'Life can little more supply,
Than just a few good Fucks, and then we die.'
John Wilkes, 'Essay on Woman' 1754

'It's a boy' or 'It's a girl' is the first observation ever made about any human being, and a very large number of other dualistic characterisations by which we describe people, concepts and the inanimate world can readily be seen to be closely derived from the basic category of gender.

The quest for loving sexual intimacy is so central a pursuit in our lives that, at any time we do not have it, we are constantly on the qui vive for a suitable other. Sexual desire and its fulfilment is the most sought after experience because the arousal as well as the fulfilment is intensely pleasurable. This is due to the unique cooperation between the sympathetic and para-sympathetic nervous systems in sexual desire, which sets it apart from all other forms of arousal and, in the right context, may be evaluated by us as the condition in life whose ecstasy rivals the fear of death in its intensity. Passionately loving sexual orgasm has been given the name *la petite mort*, the death we are more than willing to experience.

In normal circumstances we are instinctively highly selective in our choice of a mate, in favour of narcissistic self-reflection. The members of our immediate family are the first objects of our sexual desire, and incestuous fantasies and impulses are experienced in all families – between parents and children, between brothers and sisters and, not infrequently, between uncles and nieces, aunts and nephews, and grandparents and their grandchildren. However, notwithstanding the prevalence of incest amongst the morally degenerate, we are most powerfully attracted to others who are very, but not too much, like the members of our family. Even in legally sanctioned couplings of quite close relatives, such as between uncles or aunts and nieces or nephews, and between first cousins, we tend to avoid the genetic risks associated with too-close inbreeding. But our marital beds are mentally highly populated.

Isn't it amusing how often people obviously in love with each other are observably alike in colouring, overall body shape and size and especially, I notice, in idiosyncratic details of their physiognomy, from the overall shapes of their faces to nose and mouth and ear shapes to rarely placed dimples and moles.

Homosexuality may be seen as the quest for narcissistic identification taken to the limit, whereas heterosexuality adds to narcissistic identification the complex tension of conflict and attraction in the oppositeness of the genders. It seems to be the case that some people are born to be homosexual, irrespective of any conditioning to the contrary, and some people are born to be heterosexual, notwithstanding any conditioning to the contrary. Nevertheless, there is abundant evidence that a child's family experiences, especially in the Oedipal stage of development between about three and six, are – for the vast majority of people – powerfully influential in determining his or her sexual orientation.

Whether heterosexual or homosexual, the differing characteristics of the genders overwhelmingly inform the whole of our lives. *Masculinity* and *femininity* are the biological bottom line, although aspects of femininity are observable in the most heterosexual of men and aspects of masculinity are observable in the most heterosexual of women. Indeed, in many heterosexual couples, the masculinity in the woman may be particularly attracted to the femininity in the man, and vice versa. And it is noteworthy in many homosexual couples that they quickly differentiate themselves in their behaviour within their relationship into archetypally 'masculine' and 'feminine' roles.

The tensions of duality excite us, make us feel fully alive, (See 'Our Species' and 'Duality Rules, OK'), and, notwithstanding exceptions, the ditty credited to Henry James,

Hogamous higamous, men are polygamous;
Higamous hogamous, women monogamous.

is the basic source of tension between heterosexual men and women.

Despite the usual manifestations of our chosen orientation in the expression of our sexuality – be it 'straight', transvestite, narcissist, homosexual or bisexual – our sexual urges are so powerful that, in sufficiently restricted conditions, most of us would have sex with anybody of either sex or – dare it be said – even with animals. To this extent, we are pliable. But *our gender is bigger and much more inflexible than our sexual orientation.* Male and female are sex, masculine and feminine are gender, and though the conceptions overlap, they are not synonymous.

Homosexual men are identifiably of the masculine gender; lesbian women are identifiably of the feminine gender. Our gender informs more than our sexual proclivities – it pervades every aspect of our lives and is much more elusive than our sexuality.

In recent years it has become possible and permissible for many desperate people to be physiologically and anatomically (more or less) transformed from one gender into the other. (All reported cases are of people who are anatomically unambiguously the gender they want to renounce; true hermaphroditism is extremely rare.) They all avow that this is unrelated to their sexual orientation and refers only to their deep, lifelong knowledge that their anatomy is incompatible with their true gender identity, which is *immutable,* yet has still eluded definition.

In 1974, the journalist and travel writer Jan (nee James) Morris wrote, 'We are told that the social gap between the sexes is narrowing, but I can only report that having, in the second half of the 20th century, experienced life in both roles, there seems to me no aspect of existence, no moment of the day, no contact, no arrangement, no response, which is not different for men and women. The very tone of voice in which I was now addressed, the very posture of the person next in the queue, the very feel of the air when I entered a room or sat at a restaurant table, constantly emphasised my change of status.'

Whatever else transexualism implies, it certainly puts paid to the, until very recently, fashionable notion that observable differences of outlook, predispositions and behaviour between the genders are essentially conditioned rather than innate. While the vast majority of us are lucky enough to have our gender awareness and our anatomies appropriately matched, the few who do not bear incontrovertible witness to our bodies (usually) only representing our more profound, invisible gender. Where is gender located? In our brains? What in particular makes living the wrong gender so unbearable?

In the usual course of development, a child under the age of about three has no clear understanding of the immutability of their gender; and toddlers of either sex can be heard to say, interchangeably, 'When I'm a lady, like Mummy ...' or 'When I'm a man, like Daddy...' Gender awareness and proto-sexual awareness is developed in the Oedipal stage of development between the ages of about three and six. Six to twelve is the stage of withdrawal into 'latency', manifest as a preference for essentially asexual friendships with same-gender peers (although dormant heterosexual impulses are frequently observable at this stage in clandestine 'I'll show you mine if you show me yours...'). A confused homo-heterosexual genital orientation is manifest at puberty, from about twelve to sixteen, which gives way, in later adolescence, to a full, (usually) unambiguous heterosexual genital orientation.

This is when the essential conflict between men and women

begins. Boys are more powerfully testosterone-driven than they will ever be again; they are obsessed by pure physical sexuality but know nothing of romantic tenderness. Girls are driven by dreams of their wedding day and romantic happy-ever fantasies; they know little or nothing of the power of purely physical sexual passion.

By about their mid-twenties men are beginning to understand how love can enhance pure physical sexuality, and women are beginning to experience the power of sex for its own sake, but men's essential sexual orientation and women's essential love orientation remain at war throughout their lives.

Men's imperative sexual needs put them at the mercy of women, who accept or reject their advances and on whose willingness they depend. Women simply desire men's faithfulness; men complexly desire to have sex with many women *and* to be lovingly and securely cared for. Until recently, women were united in their agreement to refuse men their sexual favours until they had feminised them by transmuting their lust into love. Men protested but were secretly glad to find in marriage the best possible resolution of their conflicting desires. Notwithstanding their infidelities the vast majority of men have always chosen more or less monogamous marriage over free promiscuity, realising that untrammelled sexual freedom becomes tired and meaningless, and that in leaving a wife for a mistress the mistress quickly becomes another wife. In truth, of the four groups, married and unmarried women and married and unmarried men, bachelors are unhappier than married or single women and married men the happiest of all.

Popular received wisdom decrees that men abusively exploit women in buying their services as prostitutes, but it is actually women who exploit men in this transaction. Notwithstanding that prostitutes – male and female – are often exploited and abused by pimps they become involved with, in the simple exchange between female prostitutes and their male clients it is the women who abuse the men.

For normal, mature men (as well as women) the pleasure of sexual intercourse is incomparably enhanced when combined with emotional intimacy and, even without emotional intimacy, greatly enhanced for both parties by their awareness of the pleasure they are giving the other. For whatever reason a man is unable to get the free sex which would naturally boost his self-esteem, in his compulsively needy encounter with a prostitute she deeply humiliates him through her clear communication that he gives her no real pleasure and he is only tolerated for the money he pays her.

Maturely, both men and women seek maximum, secure guaranteed tenderness *and* high octane erotic excitement. But there is a zero-sum relation between these aims.

Traditionally, both men and women have opted for long-term tenderness over fickle eroticism, since we anticipate wanting love for many years after our sexual desire and desirability has significantly waned. Some have had their cake and eaten it through tenderly secure marriages *and* insecure, passionate erotic extra-marital liaisons. Some couples manage this arrangement well, but for most it is a dangerous mix, often resulting in the loss of both marriage partners and lovers. But however unrealistically, most of us want to be tenderly loved and passionately desired in one relationship.

The 'double standard' deplored by feminists in which women are deemed more guilty than men for sexual infidelity has some legitimacy. By and large, women are unlikely to be unfaithful unless they feel themselves to be in love, whereas men are capable of sexual congress that has no meaning beyond the act itself. Thus, some women are able to shrug off their long-term partner's infidelities, whereas men's sexual jealousy is more often unbounded.

Lately, I have noticed a trend in which couples maximise security and excitement by establishing committed monogamous relationships but abjure living together. Is this perhaps the way to get the best possible of both worlds at the same time?

Apart from the power women have over men through strategic withholding of their sexual favours, women also have the advantage of being more self-sufficient than men. While both boys and girls establish their models of emotional-sexual relating in the Oedipal stage of development, their experiences of this stage are not symmetrical. In the usual course of events both boys and girls spend far more time with their mothers than with their fathers. To the extent that her first love object – her father – 'goes to work' and spends relatively little time with her, the girl learns to be content while largely away from his presence; to the extent that she models herself on her same-sexed parent – her mother – she learns that women are 'always busy' in ways that she, later, imitates in her own life. The boy, on the other hand, spends most of his time with his first love object – his mother – and has little idea of what his father 'does' that he, too, will do in grown-up life; he is very dependent – often shamefully – on the love of his mother and very unclear about how he will identify with and imitate his father in grown-up life.

Thus, by extrapolation into adulthood, men are much more dependent on women than women are on men. Young men avow and grow their masculine self-esteem by loudly banging their bongo drums in defiance of their feared emasculation. But, in due course, they realise they also need to be useful to others to feel good about themselves, which they can best achieve by becoming breadwinners for women and their shared children. Men also value women for the comforts of *home* that women create. 'Bachelor pads' are singularly sterile and, sooner or later, most men want to return to the Nurturing Parent environment they knew in childhood. *Women's role is to tame men*. Men want to be tamed but their pride is loath to admit it; and wise women allow men their protests while gentling them into the submission they really want.

Modern sexual freedom (in the cultures we are familiar with) began in the eighteenth century in parallel with the secularisation of life. While men and women, throughout history, have flouted sexual taboos explicitly imposed on them, despite the often severe penalties for being caught doing so, it is only in the past couple of centuries that sexual freedom has been progressively enlarged – even to the present day – and acquired mainstream legitimacy. The Women's Liberation movement of the 1970s and latter-day feminism which succeeded it has endorsed sexual freedom as well as many other 'rights', especially for women.

But there is much that has been lost. The feminist movement of the past forty years has not produced a prelapsarian overcoming of 'the battle of the sexes.' There is much evidence in the media and in many books still being written of some of feminism's failures – from both men's and women's points of view. In my practice as a psychotherapist I am daily confronted with individuals who express the same old 'it's not fair' antipathies between the sexes. In the name of the quest for 'equality', many of the rejected distinctions between men's and women's roles in their families and their workplaces declare that the eternal, tense, and fruitful balance of power between the sexes has, in fact, been deleteriously undermined, with the inevitable consequence that men are increasingly reluctant to defer to marriage or even monogamous commitment. While, prima facie, this would seem to be a triumph for men, my observation is that men, too, feel undermined. Not only are contemporary men denied their biological pleasure in the thrill of the chase, they are also no longer deemed 'better than women' as breadwinners, no longer heads of households, and are, collectively, as unhappy as women were forty years ago. Out of their desolation, they are, ironically, seeking self-esteem through the narcissism that women have rejected. Men's magazines flourish, promoting face creams and lifts and clothing to make them, like women, sexually desirable objects, their only alternative seemingly being to resort to brutish laddism.

The generations that have attained adulthood in the past thirty years or so have heard about the supreme joy of loving sexual intimacy but presume this to be intrinsic to the act of sex itself rather than as the earned expression of love that has been nourished. Previous generations were protected against this misunderstanding by the moral imperatives of religious education. Now, our permissive society is the enemy of joy in denying the need for pain or shame in intimate relationships, and speciously denying the eternal battle of the sexes and the tense, exciting equilibrium of power between them achieved in the traditional arts of sexual politics.

People have always breached sexual taboos but previously, when they were disappointed in the outcome of their transgressions, they could attribute their disappointment to their failure to live up to their own ideals. Now they can only feel the pain of cynical nihilism with no prospect of redemption.

While the huge failure rate of contemporary marriages can plausibly be attributed, at least in part, to the beneficial freedom society now grants us to part without shame as previous generations could not, it is also partly attributable to the ease with which people 'have' sex. Free Child to Free Child, 'I fancy you' is very quickly consummated but, unromantically, in no way guarantees emotional (Adapted Child) and moral (Parent) compatibility.

Courtship, in the past, was the period in which couples eschewed full sexual congress but faced, full-frontally, the challenges of their emotional and familial differences and difficulties before deciding the rightness or wrongness of each other as marriage partners. Now, couples can short-circuit their inevitable antagonisms by falling into bed and, in the absence of any deeper understanding, many modern marriages are made on the basis of sexual habit. But sexual passion fades quickly, after which many couples discover that, minus the lust that brought them together, they have no compatible purposes that warrant the continuation of their relationship.

One of the particular by-products of latter-day feminism is the issue of women demanding the right to power in the institutions of religion.

In principle, religion is the spirituality that unites men and women in the mythical reunification of oppositeness that divides them. In practice, religious observance is a manifestation of the receptive, feminine being-ness in us all that opposes the active, masculine doing-ness in us all.

Men, primarily humiliated by being born out of women's wombs, have a hard time finding the balance between asserting their separateness from women and acknowledging their dependence on them. Traditionally, the officers of religion – rabbis, priests and mullahs – have been exclusively male, a wise way of feminising men while investing them with a sense of their masculine hegemony. Latter-day feminism that insists on women's rights to hold religious office is a stupid disturber of the peace. Strong female wisdom allows men their pomp, their men-only authority and pride (balancing the hegemony of women in the home), and grants them the pleasures of the pomp and ceremony, the hierarchy and the uniforms of institutionalised religion, all of which helps keep them contentedly tame. The ministry used to be one of the most respected masculine occupations; and it is surely not unconnected to the usurping of the dignified maleness of religious office that the majority of the men now seeking religious ordination are gay.

Of all the feminism-inspired political correctnesses none is so joyless as the taboo against sexism. The love-hate, push-pull of duality ambivalently seeking unity in the battle of the sexes infuses life with most of its colour and excitement. Men desire, and women desire to be desired; but no longer may a man touch or by innuendo express his desire for a woman, and no longer may a woman admit to enjoying a salacious remark or look given her by a man.

Far from undermining women, true sexism is politeness of the soul. I once memorably observed an elegant young man flirting, to her obvious delight, with an obese old woman selling him a bunch of flowers from her market stall. Men, too, deserve to be charmed and, when rejected, to be so with a gracious 'no' that is grateful rather than hostile.

There are no communities on earth that do not pointedly distinguish the genders in terms of expected psychological attitudes and roles in life as well as in terms of anatomy and physiology, no matter how different any other culture's specific stereotyping may be from our own.

Vive la difference!

Morality

Whether or not there has been or can be progress in matters pertaining to human nature is debatable. Civilisation is the usual name given to the structures of society that aim to increase the overall wellbeing of the world. But these structures seem to be eminently fragile. Regular episodic outbursts of collective, uncivilised aggression seem to increase the overall pain in the world in exact proportion to the degree of civilisation that is the current ideal. It is arguable that the sum total of pleasure and pain in the world must, because of the immutability of human nature, remain constant. As sons and daughters of Adam and Eve we are all exiles from paradise.

Our consciousness of the imperfection of our human nature and our valiant struggles to perfect ourselves sets us apart from all other species and has amongst its spin-offs all of art, science, literature and philosophy. Our morality is our quest to perfect ourselves in relation to our fellow human beings.

We are not born moral beings. Our morality (and our generalised beliefs and values) are contained in and expressed by our Parent ego state, which is mostly developed in the Oedipal stage of our development and polished up in adolescence. (See 'Ego States'). We are singular as a species in having a Parent ego state. (See 'Our Species') Our Parent ego state is our *character* (as contrasted with our Child, which is our *personality*.) It is our Parent ego state that receives *respect* from others.

Our morality is our 'goodness', the part of us that transcends the utterly self-seeking hedonism of our Child. On those occasions when we voluntarily forgo the self-centredness of our Child's wishes in favour of a moral 'good' that directly or indirectly benefits another or others, we feel *proud* of ourselves; on those occasions when we sacrifice another's or others' wellbeing in favour of our self-centredness, we are *ashamed* of ourselves. Shame is a very painful self-humiliating emotion. We are the only species that blushes.

However, there are loopholes in the rigidity of our Parent's demand for goodness. Most notably, we are generally permitted to go to any lengths to defend our personal survival. Furthermore, we are permitted to kill in war, we are permitted to lie in circumstances when we deem kindness to be a greater moral value than 'the truth', in which case it is a 'white lie'; conversely, 'A truth that's told with bad intent/ Beats all the lies you can invent'. Our crimes are less harshly judged when fuelled by passion, or when the balance of our minds is disturbed, or we are too young to know better. The hallmark of all moral matters is *mitigating circumstances*.

The laws of any society codify morality, but religion is its true guardian. Except in theocracies, morality is bigger than the laws of the land. It is not illegal for bankers to pocket their millions, but isn't it immoral? It is not illegal to walk past someone who has collapsed in the street, but isn't it immoral? Are we doing 'good' or 'bad' by giving money to a beggar we know will use it to purchase self-destructive drugs?

Granting clemency to flawed morality begins with our judgement of God, the super-duper Parent, the ultimate arbiter of right and wrong. God rewards goodness and punishes badness – except when he doesn't. If goodness was always rewarded by God and badness always punished, we would have no need of moral debate; if goodness was never rewarded and badness was never punished, we would happily become moral nihilists. But God *usually* rewards goodness and *usually* punishes badness and so, by intermittent reinforcement – the most powerful of all conditioning techniques – God teases and tantalises us into forever questing to understand his Will. (See 'The Life and Death of God').

In response to 'Where was God in Auschwitz?' some respond that his absence proves his non-existence (at least as a benevolent entity). To the determinedly religious, the response is contained in the Book of Job; who are we to judge the almighty creator whose purposes are hidden from our view but who has given us life and all the awesome wonders of the universe; we only see the tangled threads on the back of the beautiful tapestry woven by God.

Are some people born with more capacity for wrongdoing than others, and are they more 'good' if they avoid wrongdoing than those who are innately not so predisposed? Are some people so brutalised in childhood that they can't help themselves becoming brutalisers? What are society's responsibilities towards its miscreants? Should they be punished? Are they redeemable by love or only by bootcamping? Thus we are led to the eternal, indissoluble problem of fate versus free-will and all its offshoots in mundane life.

One thing is clearly established: irrespective of moral questions associated with punishment, contrary to popular belief, *punishment doesn't work*. Punishment is negative strokes and negative strokes, as well as positive strokes, re-enforce the behaviour they are given for. The mistaken belief that punishment works derives from the fact that, momentarily, while the punishment is actually being inflicted, it does inhibit the undesired behaviour.

In the mid-twentieth century, the behavioural psychologist, B. F. Skinner, in his ground-breaking experiments in training pigeons, showed that although they immediately desisted from undesired behaviour when punishment was inflicted on them, immediately afterwards, the expression of that behaviour *increased*. But through his various schedules of reinforcement (positive stroking) he was able to train his pigeons to play ping-pong! And, observation that looks beyond the facile expediency of punishment, bears witness to its inefficacy; the same children in a classroom are punished over and over again for their unapproved behaviour, and the recidivism rate of prisoners in our gaols is eighty per cent. Skinner unequivocally proved that the only way to eliminate undesirable behaviour is to *ignore it*, give it *no strokes at all – ever*. Easier said than done!

Consider a two-year-old having a temper-tantrum because she wants a chocolate biscuit and Mummy has said no. After about five minutes, Mummy can stand it no longer and gives in. The next day, the child again screams for a chocolate biscuit and Mummy again says no. The child goes on screaming, but Mummy holds out and continues to say no. After ten minutes of the child's screaming Mummy gives in, mistakenly thinking that she has 'done better' this time by holding out for longer. On the contrary, the child now knows that she needs to go on screaming for ten minutes to get what she wants; and the longer the mother holds out and then gives in, the more will the child become habituated to screaming ever-longer for what she wants. For as long as the mother doubts her ability to *never* give into her child's screaming for what she wants, she is best advised to give in *immediately*. Then, when the mother is confident of her ability to *never* again give in, the child will get the message very quickly. The pain, for trainer and trained, can be mitigated by rewards (positive strokes) that are given – again *immediately* – for desisting from the undesired behaviour.

Could we not train our judges, our teachers, our prison warders, our probation officers, and our foreign secretaries to understand and deploy these unambiguously established psychological truths? How about the United States saying to Israel and the Palestinians, 'If you two don't stop fighting, we're withdrawing your pocket money' (and meaning it)?

In our bids to be 'good' and avoid the wrath of God and, by extrapolation, the wrath of our parents and other authorities to whom we defer, there are two components of our nature that we deploy: our Adapted Child and our Parent. The vast majority of the religiously observant population of the world is obedient through its Adapted Child. Our Adapted Child is mindlessly obedient, essentially out of *fear of retribution* and, secondarily, in order to be *righteous* and so expectant of reward, at least in the world to come. This Adapted Child righteousness is what gives meaning and value to the lives of the nearly starving, the illiterate, and otherwise suffering multitudes in the world. But the Adapted Child's relationship to God is one of *Trying Hard* (See 'The Enemies of Love'); its promises to God are inevitably broken with transgressions which invoke the fear of losing its eternal happiness in the world to come and, indeed, being cast eternally into hell.

All religions have constructed devices that enable us to be redeemed from damnation for our flawed goodness. Roman Catholicism, in particular, eases the anguish of billions of its superstitious and fearful adherents, with its construct of confession and associated 'penances' (willingly accepted negative strokes) that clear the decks and grant permission to sin again, pay penance again ... forever sinning but making sure that at the end of this life the slate is wiped clean in readiness for eternal happiness.

Religious observance that is expressed through our Parent ego state is rare and, by and large, limited to the literate, educated and contemplative adherents of any religion. Its faith does not eschew, but welcomes questioning, is flexible, tolerant and inspired by awe; its piety is informed by love rather than fear of God and all his creation. It is the ideal of all religions.

An interesting mundane Adapted Child derivative of religious 'goodness' is 'political correctness', which invokes rigid adherence to the notion of our equal love for all other human beings. In the name of avoiding *prejudice* (Parent-Adult contamination) it disallows any admission of purely Adult awareness of differences between people that interest and amuse us. Expression of such awareness is now taboo but, like all Adapted Child restraints, it is mindless obedience without substantive justification; it increases rather than diminishes our intolerance of human differences. Real tolerance of others comes from the precepts taught to our Parent ego state, and is not incompatible with the affectionate teasing of each other for our differences. What misplaced do-gooding denies us, for example, are the pleasures of those delightful television series like *Rising Damp* and *Beggar Thy Neighbour*.

One component of our moral debates and judgements is that of *motive*. Many sound moral judgements can only be made in the context of the known intention of the perpetrator of an act.

A standard test of the moral maturity of a child is to pose a question like, 'Michael reaches in the cupboard for some sweets he is not supposed to eat and knocks a plate off the shelf, breaking it. Peter is helping his Mummy set the table for lunch. He accidentally trips and breaks three plates. Which boy is the naughtiest?' Children under the age of about eight answer Peter.

In 2001, Harold Shipman, a medical practitioner, was found guilty of murdering more than two hundred of his patients by injecting them with lethal doses of morphine. The ensuing inquiry concluded that 'the motivation for his murders is incomprehensible *and* he is an incontrovertibly evil man'. In the light of the first half of this judgement, I maintain that the second half cannot be vouchsafed. We may justifiably call his actions evil but, without knowing his motive, can we justifiably call the *man* evil?

At the time of Shipman's widely reported trial I became fascinated by some of the revealed details of his life that prompted me to speculate about his motive for his murders. When he was eighteen, Shipman witnessed his mother's agonising death from cancer, from which trauma he admitted he had never recovered. Most of his patients whom he murdered were elderly women, many of them seriously ill.

Psychologically speaking, we know that, largely unconsciously and informed by a complex mixture of innate temperament and circumstantial early experiences, all human beings are motivated by a personal agenda that aims to give their lives overall meaning and significance. Particular traumatic experiences in childhood are often the key to accessing an individual's central lifelong heroic quest. (See 'The Quest for Happiness')

So, in the case of Harold Shipman, I hypothesise that the central trauma of his life may explain his multiple murders. That is, I suggest his lifelong motivation was to free himself of the trauma of his mother's death by re-writing his personal history. His gentle, painless killings of his usually elderly female patients were all bids to make his mother die painlessly. And the relatively few male patients he murdered could have been stand-ins for himself in a subsidiary bid to end his own suffering. (He was widely appreciated for his undisputed kindness and gentleness as a GP).

Well, of course, my hypothesis is unprovable. There may be many other equally plausible motivational hypotheses attributable to Harold Shipman, and the man himself never declared his motive. But if, for argument's sake, my hypothesis were correct, would our condemnation of the man (but not his deeds) be mitigated? Would this make him 'good' but mad, or 'evil' but forgivable? I propose that the attribution 'evil person' should be limited to a description of the contents of some people's Parent ego state. Hitler's deeds were evil, but Hitler, the man, was also evil because he had evil beliefs.

And motive aside, can we quantify the 'badness' of an individual's deeds? If the Yorkshire Ripper murdered twenty women and Harold Shipman murdered two hundred, were Harold Shipman's crimes exactly ten times more evil? What does God think about these things? These questions are, of course, what priests, rabbis and mullahs peruse.

As recently as fifty years ago the Western affluent societies we are familiar with were discernibly more bound by religious observance than they are today. And this was reflected in the consensual validation of many of our basic Parent values. Virtually all children were respectful of all adults, and all adults were free publicly to reprimand any children seen behaving badly, which most adults wouldn't dare to do now. And it is statistically the case that most adults were more honest than they are today. Although humanism avows its sufficiency to maintain morality in the name of enlightened self-interest, the evidence is that this is not so.

Until recently, Religious Education, which taught morality, was a mandatory part of every school curriculum; it no longer is. It seems to be the case that, without religion, morality in general is declining in its hold on large segments of the population. The gangs of murderously angry (Try Hard/Hurry Up – see 'Compound Personality Types') youths that maraud in our cities bear witness to their members' untutored, undeveloped Parent ego states. Ironically, they are violent towards others who 'disrespect' them, thus unwittingly declaring the vacuum in them that should be filled by the moral values that invoke the esteem of others as well as what we usually mean by 'self-confidence'. Religious fundamentalism is the unappetising contemporary backlash against moral nihilism. What else can restore the equilibrium between self-centredness and morality that is so essential to our wellbeing that so many have lost with the demise of God?

The Quest for Happiness

'They strive after happiness, they want to become happy and to remain so ... on the one hand, as an absence of pain and displeasure and, on the other, as the experiencing of strong feelings of pleasure... What we call happiness in the strictest sense comes from the (preferably sudden) satisfaction of needs which have been dammed up to a high degree, and it is from its nature only possible as an episodic phenomenon. When any situation that is desired by the pleasure principle is prolonged it only produces a feeling of mild contentment. We are so made that we can derive enjoyment only from a contrast and very little from a state of things.' Freud

Striving for the optimal balance between order and chaos, rest and busyness, the fear of death and the quest for excitement, discipline and spontaneity, is the volatile, unremitting biological quest of the whole of our lives, whether we are conscious of it or not.

Psychologically, life is sophistry, and the principal trick we are bound to deploy is to live life as if it *matters*, despite the mockery that death makes of all our concerns.

Religions offer general meanings that are applicable to everybody. Atheists and agnostics may reject any doctrinaire general meaning of life associated with a Will higher than our own; but everybody has some general meaning they give to life even if it be as cynically reductionist as 'Every man for himself.'

Each human being also has his own personal meanings by which he seeks to make his individual life significant and creates myths in which he or she is the hero or heroine. That is, all human beings make decisions about the progressive 'becoming' of their lives as well as decisions about their ways of 'being' in the world. Our personal meanings of life include what we will actively do to unfold our potential and fulfil our dreams, as well as what kinds of attitudes and responses we will have to other people. Our 'being' decisions refer to survival and love; our 'becoming' decisions refer to achievement and love. Love of particular others for what we *are* and the love of people in general ('fame and fortune' for our worldly achievements) have timelessly been the hoped-for panacea against the inevitability of our deaths. The prospect of death can, paradoxically, be diminished as we get closer to it, if we are able to perceive ourselves as having fulfilled our idiosyncratic potential in the realms of loving intimacy and of significance in our work and its achievements.

The pursuit of our quest for individual significance propels us into a mythical projection of life as a process towards a golden, perfected future. Consciously or unconsciously, crudely or with refinement, we are all artists, creating and re-creating the picture that will coherently tell the triumphant story of our lives. We create our lives retrospectively, when a certain distance enables us to see episodes of the past as distinct pieces of the jigsaw puzzle we are putting together to make the picture of our lives. A completed patch of our jigsaw puzzle may give us enough to guess, by extrapolation, what the whole picture is about, but we may have to change our minds as we proceed. We make mistakes when we try to squeeze the wrong piece of experience or the wrong person into a particular place and the artist in us is then ashamed and seeks to negate our folly.

We want our picture to be perfectly finished before we die. Thus, everything that happens to us objectively is either experienced as significant by virtue of its symbolic relevance to the ongoing story of our lives, or else is rejected as 'noise'. Our metaphors mediate between our consciousness and external reality. Each person's pursuit of the fulfilment of his own myths is his truth; everything else is, for him, irrelevant and, therefore, of no intrinsic interest. Man is a symbolic animal and, though only few may articulate this fact, everybody lives it.

The existence of any attribute of a thing or person necessarily implies an opposite attribute that also exists. There is no 'up' without 'down', no 'good' without 'evil', no sound of a left hand clapping. (See 'Duality Rules, OK') Thus the wish to progress towards the fulfilment of our triumphant dreams implies the fear that we may progress towards the fulfilment of our coexisting tragic nightmares. At any time in our lives, in our work and our intimate relationships, we are making our dreams or our nightmares, or both, come true. Fear of our nightmares inhibits us in the quest for our dreams. But we can only overcome our fears through the process of working courageously towards the fulfilment of our dreams even while we are frightened. Hamlet was one level removed from the truth; in the beginning was cowardice, conscience is its justification.

By and large, our myths contain two distinct, although often overlapping themes: how we will 'succeed' in the world at large, broadly based on our 'unfinished business' with our same-sexed parent; and how we will be loved by our chosen sexual partner, broadly based on our 'unfinished business' with our opposite-sexed parent.

Our unfinished business with our same-sexed parent concerns the aggrandisement of our power, which, inasmuch as it refers to our self-esteem, involves our sense of worthiness in having our dream of love fulfilled; but it is principally focused on the achievement of our status in the world at large, through what we do. Our unfinished business with our opposite-sexed parent concerns the fulfilment of our dream of being loved for who we are.

'Doing' is the masculine principle in us all; 'being' is the feminine principle in us all. So, by and large, men feel themselves unready for the fulfilment of love until their masculine self-esteem is assured by some measure of worldly accomplishment; and, by and large, women feel themselves unready wholeheartedly to pursue careers until their feminine self-esteem is assured through loving and being loved by a man. But in the long run, men need to 'be' as well as 'do' and women need to 'do' as well as 'be' in order to be wholesome human beings, and healthy intimacy can only flourish between two distinctively whole people.

It is in the development of spirituality associated with the quest for meaning in life that men and women can each reach successfully beyond the attractions and antipathies between the genders to a higher level of living that encompasses masculinity and femininity and unites individual men and women in their common humanity. Broadly speaking, feeling and intuiting (the Child) is the femininity in us all, thinking and knowing-how (the Adult) is the masculinity in us all, and believing (the Parent) is the humanity in us all.

Access to our myths is through childhood memory. In childhood, unconstrained by all the sophistication of grown-up 'realism', we unashamedly allowed ourselves to be fully conscious of and free and open in expressing our dreams of fulfilment. In response to the wry question adults so often ask of children, 'What are you going to be when you grow up?', the answer we gave usually referred to our achievement in the world at large.

Our dreams of love with an intimate other are subtler and, even in childhood, were tainted by shame that prevented us from fully admitting them to ourselves or others. Our shame of our dream of love was proportional to the degree of deviation of that dream from the ideal: 'When I grow up I am going to be a lady/man just like Mummy/Daddy and marry a man/lady just like Daddy/Mummy.' Deviation of our dream of love from the ideal represents the fact we did not feel fully loved by our parents and did not fully love them in return. (See 'Personality Types') And we knew, even in childhood, that grown-ups demanded that we only believe and only utter the acceptable 'truth' that we and our parents loved each other wholeheartedly. Except in the rare instances where the child actually experiences the relationships of her parents to each other and to herself as being very close to the ideal, all children indoctrinate themselves with the untruth based on the false propriety imposed on them, by virtue of which they are bound to live their nightmares as well as their dreams in their grown-up intimate relationships.

Revivifying and fully articulating our childhood dreams of achievement and love not only gives us the confidence of knowing where we are aiming but also gives us the intrinsic satisfaction of perceiving ourselves as creative artists. Knowing our dreams enables us to incorporate our memories into them. Without this facility our memories are dissociated and fragmented meaningless episodes, which recur with seeming fatality, until we imbue them with significance.

Desire seeks its fulfilment in pleasure, but pleasure is not guaranteed. Intrinsic to the process is the risk of failure and an associated degree of pain equivalent to the pleasure sought. But all pleasure and pain depends on our *beliefs* about them. When significance is added, we can be glad and proud of our remembered pains as well as our joys, all of which can then be experienced as parts of the artistic plan of our lives, of which we are directors. The past is constantly available to us for re-remembering and reinterpreting for the purpose of unfolding and refining our lives as works of art. It is the *courage and the struggle* truthfully to live out our personal myths that is the measure of a man's or woman's worth. Doing what we most fear even while we are frightened is courageous, creative living. As Nietzsche put it, 'One thing is needful to "give style" to one's character – a great and rare art! It is practised by those who survey all the strengths and weaknesses of their nature and then fit them into an artistic plan until every one of them appears as art and reason and even weaknesses delight the eye.'

As hero or heroine of our personal myth, the process of our lives is toward the triumph of fulfilment and the serenity at the end of our lives when, retrospectively, everything we have experienced can be seen, without sanctimonious piety, to have been an essential part of our life plan, neither good nor bad but simply the way it had to be for us. The extent of a person's creative courage is not readily seen, and the extent of his or her outer world achievements is irrelevant. It is only in loving sexual intimacy that we may learn to know another person, and ourselves be known, at the mythic centre of our beings.

We are all locked in the cages constructed out of that complex amalgam of nature and nurture that has made us what we are, but we are free to paint the bars of our cages in the colours of our choosing. Our responses are our choices. Happy genes and a contented childhood are the lot of some who, consequently live simple and contented lives. Innate psychological or physical handicaps and a sorry childhood are the lot of others who, consequently are beset with angst or live lives of creative peaks and troughs beyond the capacity of the simply contented. Without our neurotic compulsions associated with our uniquely human consciousness of self, there would be no despair and no exultation.

Our responses to our fates are our choices, and these have consequences. We cannot avoid making choices. Passivity is the self-delusion of 'no choice'; but, of course, it is a choice and like all others has consequences. Every moment of choice is the cause of the inexorable train of events that follows in its wake, to the natural conclusion of a 'happening' in our lives. When a conclusion is painful we are loath to remember the moment of choice that determined it, although repression can never be complete, and often the knowledge that we have chosen a path to pain is manifest as an obsessive fear of that pain, too late, and an obsessive struggle to avoid it.

We have three broad choices of response to our fates: 1) resentful envy – being five feet tall and wanting only to be an

Olympic high-jumper; 2) passive, unambitious acceptance – having a beautiful voice but never getting any training and singing only in the shower; and 3) creative struggle – stretching the boundaries of our being to fulfil *the nearly but not quite impossible*, which gives us the greatest possible satisfaction (from the epic, like Michelangelo painting the ceiling of the Sistine Chapel, to the trivial, like a housewife adding a cup of water to a pan of soup in order to cater for an unexpected guest).

Most people live by the mutually contradictory beliefs that they choose freely, moment by moment, to behave as they wish *and* that when they are frustrated in their desires it is because they are 'unlucky'. In truth, luck – good and bad – can rarely be ascribed to anything more important that just catching or just missing a bus and, in such cases, the 'good' and the 'bad' cancel each other out very quickly. The evidence from people who win the lottery and from those who are severely injured and permanently handicapped thereafter is that, within a year of their good and bad luck, they have returned to their previously experienced level of contentment or dissatisfaction with their lives.

We have no choice in the hands we are dealt. God holds the pack, which contains the totality of all that is possible. No hand is intrinsically 'better' or 'worse' than any other; playing out a grand slam with a fistful of court cards and trumps can be as boring as playing an adroitly skilful game with no trumps or court cards can be joyful.

Each hand may be likened to and contrasted with any other hand in a large number of ways, the ways chosen being determined by relevance to the game being played at any time.

We are free to choose the games we will play; and we are free to play our chosen games lightly or seriously, with desultoriness or enthusiasm, with attention or absent-mindedness, with good or bad grace, with clumsiness or artistry.

Shall we only play games where our own hand grants us a head-start towards winning? Or sometimes choose to play games where the below-average value of our hand grants us the pleasure of challenging us to stretch the boundaries of our innate limitations? Shall we learn to play one game supremely well? Or enjoy the variety of learning and playing a number of games with limited skill in each? Shall we play for high stakes or low? Shall we play games of high chance or high skill? In all these matters we are free to choose and are responsible for the consequences of our choices.

Seated across the table from our partners, what must we do to make the game as pleasurable as possible for both of us? We need explicitly to establish with our partners the conventions by which we will covertly communicate to each other the contents of our respective hands; sort our cards and categorise them in a way that makes sense within the rules of the game; make sure we have all our cards in our hand and none is hidden behind another; ascertain the strengths and weaknesses of our hand and communicate them to our partner, within the rules of the game; attend carefully to our partner's communications to us, sorting out the components of his communication into responses to us and the information he is also giving us about his own strengths and weaknesses; arrive at a mutually agreed explicit contract; play the game cooperatively, attentively, and with finesse and pleasure; apologise for any errors we make, and happily forgive our partner his or her errors, with good sportsmanship derived from our knowledge that we are both 'only human' and it is 'only a game'.

We are physically and psychologically bound by the limits of what we are, and it is as stupidly futile to waste our energy in wishing to be psychologically other than what we are as it is to wish to be the other gender, have different coloured eyes, or be a different height from the one we are. But for each of us, within our circumscriptions, there is a unique heroic story wanting to be told. That story was vivid to each of us in the honesty of childhood, when we saw life in all its imaginative essence. Our grown-up lives are inevitably cluttered by pragmatic necessities that, if we let them, so overwhelm our consciousness that we simply plod through life as purgatory and cynically dismiss as 'romantic fiction' the passion and the heroism we have lazily renounced. We need to lift the veils of pragmatism and expediency that cloud our vision, to re-discover our dream of glory and 'selfishly' pursue the path to its fulfilment; to make ourselves artists and our lives the beautiful outcome of our artistry, to which satisfaction we are inherently entitled.

We create the world with our thoughts. Out of the amorphous clay of the universe in which we exist, we sculpt the forms that give our lives meaning: experiences, ideas, and 'other people' that are joyful and painful, beautiful and ugly, good and evil. Because we are human, we are glad to accept responsibility for the joy and beauty and good in our lives, but prefer to perceive the pain and ugliness and bad in our lives as fortuitously 'happening' to us or involuntarily imposed on us by other people. Denial and projection are the chief devices by which we preserve the inherent narcissism of our fragile egos.

Loving our neighbours as we love ourselves can only be meritorious if our love for ourselves is authentic rather than a wily mask for hate. Out of being true to our own deepest myths we love ourselves. Mundanely, out of Be Perfect come guilt and organisation, out of Be Strong come rebuffs and resilience, out of Please come misunderstandings and flexibility, out of Try Hard come failures and persistence, out of Hurry Up come fears and efficiency.

When Be Perfect in us says, 'I'll do my very best and will be happy with the result,' when Hurry Up says, 'Although it is impossible to get unconditional love, conditional love is well worth having', when Please says, 'I care about other people's feelings and wishes but ultimately I will choose for myself', when Try Hard says, 'No matter that this fails, I know that by persisting I will succeed in the end', and when Be Strong says, 'No matter that I am rejected, I know that by daring I will get the love I long for in the end', then it becomes possible for us to help others, as well as ourselves, renounce our chosen paths to our nightmares. It takes only a little attentiveness to reassure Be Perfect that there is nothing to worry about, to reassure Hurry Up that there is loads of time, to thank Please for what she has done for us, to reassure Try Hard that 'you can't win 'em all' but to encourage her to 'have a go', and to express appreciation to Be Strong for her thoughtfulness.

The heroic path is not the easy choice; it wouldn't be heroic if it were. There are dragons to be slain, and our confrontations with our personal dragons are frighteningly fraught with the possibilities of danger and pain. Most people prefer to live myopically, disdaining and discounting the dragons and heroes and heroines in their own Child as childish. But the heroic path is the one that gives optimum satisfaction in this little interval in eternity we call life.

The Issue of Astrology

By and large in the Western cultures we are familiar with, the only people who heed astrology are the very small group of cognoscenti, and the semi-literate, who mindlessly read 'their stars' in the daily red tops and popular magazines. Only a very small group of intelligent and educated people are open to testing the tenets of astrology through their own experience.

Nevertheless, there are few who do not know their 'sun signs' and some of the psychological characteristics associated with them. And such personality descriptors as 'mercurial', 'martial' and 'saturnine' are ingrained in language as testimonies to the tenacity of astrological/psychological concepts.

The educated middle classes generally simply dismiss astrology as a load of superstitious hogwash; but there are a few high-IQ bigots who, aware that astrology has always been, and is, taken seriously by some eminently sober thinkers, see fit to dismiss it with a vehemence that suggests they have a powerful need to do so.

In the first place, these bigots seek to justify their scorn on two facile, supposedly rational grounds: that the precession of the equinoxes invalidates the astrological signs; and that the world cannot meaningfully be divided into twelve signs.

The precession of the equinoxes (which astrologers know all about) is irrelevant to Western astrology, which is *not* based on the popularly named clusters of stars, but on the abstract division of the ecliptic, with zero degrees Aries beginning, by definition, at the spring equinox.

Concerning the sun-sign delineations of popular columns, dividing the world into twelve is a general, but not useless, division. (In the context of public lavatories, dividing the world into two categories only is both useful and sufficient!) Daily sun-sign forecasts – if written by astrologers – are valid, but as general as a weather forecast that might say, 'Tomorrow will be hot and sunny. Dark-skinned people will be in their element, light-skinned people should stay indoors.'

Those who reject astrology out of hand can be divided into two groups: the irreligious, who fearfully dismiss it because they presume it to be fatalistic, and thus a denial of their precious free-will; and the religious, who angrily dismiss it as evil and blasphemous in its prophetic aspects. Both of these justifications for turning away from astrology are facilely specious and based on closed-minded ignorance.

Scratch just below the surface of the closed-minded disdain of astrology by the educated bigot and you discover terror. The terror is that astrology can forecast death and all the derivative mundane pains of life for an individual, which facts people do not want to know. But this terror also implies an actual deep belief in the pre-determinism of events, because those people who truly believe in 'free-will' could listen to the predictions of astrology with indifference rather than with intense hostility.

What might partly account for the dismissal of astrology as a pagan religion is the popular assumption that it is a belief system. Astrology is not 'believed in' any more than a telephone is; both are used because they work. All astrologically based choices and decisions are no more than extensions of sailing with the tide, planting by the seasons, and forecasting rain from the configurations of the clouds, all of which bear witness to our ordinary knowledgeable 'belief in' the connections between extra-terrestrial events and events on earth.

But it is impossible to study astrology without being infected by non-specific religious awe at the order and meaning in the universe and appreciation of even the smallest details of our lives as manifestations of the working of the whole, of the interconnectedness of all things and events, of each human being as a manifestation of God (or the Final Cause), of everything being the way it has to be, and of the beauty of each moment in its unique blending of hourly, monthly, yearly and epochal cycles.

For open-minded sceptics among my readers, I hope this essay will dispel commonplace objections to astrology as well as being enlightening concerning astrology's true nature.

The first basic assumption of astrology is that anything that comes into existence maintains, for the whole of its existence, the qualities of the moment it came into being, which moment can be described by the configuration of the heavens at that date and time and as seen from that place. (The coming into existence of a human being is taken to be the moment the child takes its first breath.) While, in principle, all the stars in the heavens are part of the description of a moment, for an observer on Earth, the configurations of our solar system are overwhelmingly powerful.

Astrology comprehends that in some way, not yet fully understood, the planetary configurations at the time of birth of any entity remain imprinted in that entity, even though the configurations at the moment of birth are only momentarily extant.

The horoscope is like an algebraic equation with a virtually unlimited number of 'arithmetical' solutions, and can be applied to any entity – animate or inanimate – that the human mind is capable of conceptualising: a dog, a human being, an accident, a country, a war, the weather, the start of a business, a bright idea... but the effective interpretation of the horoscope depends, at least to some extent, on the expertise of the interpreter in some mundane subject-matter. For a valuable psychological interpretation of a horoscope, the astrologer needs to be a trained psychologist, for medical matters a doctor, for a stock market analysis an economist, for weather forecasting a meteorologist, etc., although the interpretation of the natal horoscopes of human beings is by far the most popular use of astrology.

The planets and their geometrical configurations with each

other are the core significators, modified by their zodiacal signs and their placements within the horoscope.

The other basic assumption of astrology is that *the birth chart unfolds* in response to various ways in which the natal chart is 'progressed', because the birth chart is *potential – a task* to be fulfilled in the lifetime, as well as being a map of innate characteristics and predispositions.

As the planets keep moving continuously in their spheres, throughout our lives they form significant geometrical configurations to the sensitive points in our personal horoscopes. We experience these energetic 'transits' in a wide variety of ways, depending on which planet is doing the transiting and which planet or other sensitive point in our horoscope is being transited, and whether the configurations formed are basically challenging or easeful.

The Moon forms every possible transit to each individual's horoscope every month; to this extent the Moon's transits are associated with our fleeting moods. On the other hand, each of us in our lifetime is likely to experience only a handful of Pluto transits; but these are felt as life-changing directions in our lives, often spread out over a number of years. In between, the transits of the Sun, Mercury, Venus, Mars, Saturn, Chiron, Uranus and Neptune affect us with increasing power proportional to the transiting planet's length of orbit round the Sun.

A human being, an accident, a business, an earthquake, an idea, that all come into being on the same date and at the same time and place will have identical horoscopes, but the astrologer will give these entities appropriately different readings. The algebraic equation of a horoscope has as many solutions as there are entities it represents.

But no matter to what it is applied, what makes astrology special is its deep and comprehensive understanding of the interconnectedness of things and events beyond the capacity of any other language to encompass.

Nothing but astrology can see the equivalence of gas leaks, a sea voyage, film-making, anaesthesia, alcoholism and mystical transcendence; of underground explosions, survival, demagoguery and psychological transformation; of electricity, independence, intuition, homosexuality, computing and democracy; of bones, concrete, fear, self-discipline, endurance and old age; of obesity, good investments, long-distance travel, lawyers, publishers and religion; of red blood cells, iron, sexuality and accidents; of jewellery, sociability, justice, lust and good taste; of reasoning, nervousness, telephones and versatility; of feelings, femininity, childhood, gynaecology and change-ability; of ambition, pride, masculinity and the heart.

From the symbolic meanings of the sun, moon and planets, qualified by their configurations with each other and their zodiacal placements and positions in the horoscope, the *singularity of the cosmos* can be apprehended.

The interpretation of a horoscope, and prediction on it, is an art as well as a science and involves the 'educated best guesses' of the astrologer in accordance with his or her knowledge of the paths that the person is already embarked on. Most astrologers can also give remarkably accurate 'blind' readings, but even such readings are made with a lot of subliminal information, including the person's sex, age and culture.

The natal horoscope of a human being is a map of his or her genetic inheritance. Within these bounds, the native may freely choose to fulfil or to discount their potential. We are no more bound by our natal horoscopes than we are bound by our obvious genetically determined attributes, such as the colour of our eyes, our gender, our blood group, and the multitude of 'programmes' manifest in such occurrences as our acquisition of teeth, the onset of puberty, and the greying of our hair. A man four feet six inches tall would be simply foolish to deny that he will not be an Olympic high-jumper. How much energy he wastes, and how much pain he would cause himself with this ambition – energy he could use productively and pain he could avoid if only he aimed for what is actually possible for him. In exactly this way – and at deeper and subtler levels as well – astrology tells us just such truths about ourselves.

Astrology transcends our dualistic concept of 'good' and 'bad'. So-called 'bad' aspects in our horoscopes are as capable of granting great productivity and satisfaction in life as so-called 'good' aspects are capable of expression as lethargy and boredom. The patterns are determined but, with instinct enhanced by the wisdom of astrology, we are free to choose the *levels* – physical, emotional, intellectual and spiritual – at which these patterns will manifest in our lives, and we are free to choose the *attitudes* we will have to them.

Predicatively, astrology can be enormously valuable for informing us when present difficulties will pass and when desired and planned future events will probably be actualised, thus inducing in us increased patience, acceptance and serenity. 'Bad' things, 'good' things, and prediction of death are not the remit of astrology. Astrology delineates configurations of *energy* which, within the context of an individual's life, can be freely used or abused.

Life is full of alternatives within the constraints of determinism, and potentiality does not guarantee actuality. Consulting a railway timetable does not imply the necessity of catching or missing a train. Acorns may grow into oak trees; some do, some don't. Astrologically speaking, for example, some Neptune configurations suggest a vulnerability to alcoholism and/or spirituality; a whisky priest may be a hopeless drunk *and* a truly devout man. Some Mars configurations suggesting bloodshed may manifest equally plausibly in a butcher, a surgeon or a murderer. Who can say that a tall and athletic man will choose to use these endowments to be a basketball player, a high-jumper, a nightclub bouncer, a mugger, a policeman ... or not use these attributes at all? But once we know he is a basketball player we can readily see the characteristics that enabled him to become one. Astrology is as complex as life itself; if it weren't it wouldn't be true.

No astrologer worthy of the title imposes unsolicited predictions onto other people, thus falsely projecting onto another's consciousness thoughts that are not synchronous with the other's being. But once a question is voiced, the astrologer has the ability to complete the question with an answer consonant with the question's meaning for the questioner, enabling the individual to move on to another moment, unhampered by 'unfinished business' from the past.

Astrology cannot predict with *certainty* any particular manifestation in an individual's life or in the mundane world of events. But we can use the x's and y's of astrology to enhance our ability to comprehend the past and the present, and to help our future wishes to be actualised by choosing amongst the options available to us within the bounds of the pre-determined energies operating in our lives.

With or without astrology, we are all making predictions (short-term) and prophecies (longer-term) all the time, by logically projecting our knowledge of present events along the line they are already travelling. *We make predictions every time we use the future tense.*

Nearing home after a family outing, the child says, 'Rover will be pleased to see us.' Planning a dinner party we say, 'We must invite David and Susan to meet each other, they'll get on famously.' Our predictions are sometimes mistaken, but also often realised. Short-term predictions generally have best chances of success because of the relatively few unexpected events that can intervene between now and then. Sometimes we break appointments we have made because 'unforeseen circumstances' arise, but astrology enables us to predict with more confidence than unaided instinct normally allows. Every moment of Now is the necessary consequence and culmination of every previous moment in history, but was only a probability, however great, until it occurred. Our uncertainties keep us hopefully on our toes. Market research has revealed that the two most often cited reasons people give for reading newspapers are for the weather forecast and their horoscopes!

Because the future, notwithstanding the best possible predictions, remains open, it is arguable that the greatest value of astrology lies in the understanding and appreciation it offers us of the past, which is already manifest.

Nevertheless, when our concerned preoccupations are narrowly focused, predictive astrology can be enormously valuable in informing us when present difficulties are likely to pass and when desired and planned future events will probably be actualised. When will my house, which has been on the market for six months, find a buyer? When will my present financial difficulties ease? When is the best time for nudging my reluctant lover into commitment? Should I change my career now and, if not now, when? When is a good time in the next six months for me to have elective surgery? are all questions that an astrologer may confidently answer to particular clients.

The origins of astrology are lost in antiquity, but there seems to have been no country or early form of civilised community where astrology was not developed. The date of the first individual horoscope is unknown, but certainly by Greek times it had reached recognisable form, and Hippocrates maintained that no doctor was qualified if he could not interpret a patient's horoscope. For primitive man – and indeed for modern man up until about five hundred years ago – nothing was inanimate. The validity of astrology was never questioned since it was completely consistent with every human being's acceptance of himself and his life as participating in the life of nature as a whole.

There was no real distinction between astrology and

astronomy. Even at the start of the Renaissance scientists such as Copernicus, Brahe and Kepler, whose work revolutionised our view of the solar system, actively used astrology. Kepler detailed weather forecasts based on astrology as well as undertaking work for individuals, and Newton wrote far more on alchemy (which incorporates astrological symbolism) than he ever wrote on physics.

Until the rise of scientific materialism in the seventeenth century, astrology's truth was never questioned.

However, by the beginning of the twentieth century science could apparently account for everything in materialistic terms. Copernicus, Darwin and Freud had seen to it that the earth was no longer the centre of the universe, man no longer a special species and, indeed, not even able to know the depths of his own mind. Thus God – in man's image – sitting, super-powerful on a throne in the sky, was undermined. So too was astrology, which became increasingly marginal and unrespectable.

But materialistic physics has had its day. In the course of the past century the existential consequences of Heisenberg's uncertainty principle, Einstein's theory of relativity, Black Holes and chaos theory have permeated the everyday consciousness of very large numbers of people, leaving us collectively in a state of nihilistic anxiety. The theories of modern quantum physics are beginning to demonstrate a remarkable similarity with astrological ideas, especially with regard to the behaviour of sub-atomic particles which are now seen to behave as if information is being transmitted across space instantaneously, which is very close indeed to the astrological paradigm.

Perhaps the time is not far off when mankind will achieve, with the aid of astrology, a new transcendental holistic reality that displaces the mind/matter duality bequeathed to us by Descartes.

My own awakening to astrology was unsolicited. I had been, for several years, a psychotherapist trained in the vernacular of Transactional Analysis and steeped and firmly rooted in Freudian assumptions and concepts. Daily, in my work, I experienced the tangible and metaphorical consequences of the imprinted experiences of the first few years of our lives, and especially the profoundly formative influence of the Oedipus complex, which not only moulds the shape of our sexual propensities but is also a critical determiner of our world views. I loved my work and believed in the psychoanalytic assumption of Locke's tabula rasa description of the newborn mind. I acknowledged genetics, but saw its power and influence as limited to the determination of only our grossest attributes (in which belief I was in accord with the then fashionable view of the primacy of nurture over nature).

Then, one day in 1978, a man who had been in one of my therapy groups for two years came to a session and said he had just consulted an astrologer and had made a tape recording of that meeting, and please would I listen to it. Very sceptically, but indulgently, I agreed and turned it on and listened to it with half an ear while attending also to the late afternoon cacophony of my children and their demands. Within five minutes I was astounded. The astrologer, with no knowledge of my patient other than his date, place and time of birth had already said everything about him – and more – that it had taken me two years of laborious analysis to uncover. I consulted the same astrologer for myself and was overwhelmed by the authenticity and depth of what he told me about my life experiences.

In the following weeks and months I devoured shelves of books on astrology. Everything seemed changed. But I was also embarrassed by myself and, notwithstanding that I had to earn my living, I seriously considered that, in all conscience, I could not continue the hypocrisy of practising as a psychotherapist. Genetics (astrology) determined everything; the supposed influence of early childhood experiences was a total lie.

But I eventually found my own reconciliation of nature and nurture (see 'Realities') and have since happily used both psychoanalytic theory and astrology, in parallel rather than in combat, in my psychotherapeutic practice.

Many astrologers are indifferent to the fact that astrology has not yet been 'proven'; but I am one who very much wants astrology to find reconciliation with the contemporary scientific paradigm, and its validity demonstrated.

In theory, and ironically, contemporary physics is more compatible with astrology than it was with Newtonian physics, although Newton was an astrologer. The physical premise of astrology, that forces are transmitted without attenuation with increased distance and do not vary with respect to the differences of masses of planets from which they originate, is inconsistent with Newtonian mechanics; but it is completely in accord with Einstein's photo-electric theory, which demonstrates that the effect of a photon does not diminish with distance. And modern chemistry and biology emphatically describe the properties of substances in terms of architectural configurations of the atoms within molecules, which is also analogous to astrological thought.

No longer does science avow the existence of absolute objective reality, irrespective of the distortions of our perception of it, but rather that perceiver and perceived are inextricably linked in the actuality of what is. It now seems that the functioning of the universe is 'synchronistic', the idea first espoused by Carl Jung of a-causal connectedness between happenings that, from the point of view of our rational, conscious minds, are inexplicable.

Dr Percy Seymour, lecturer in astronomy at Plymouth University, proposes that, in a sense, we are all natural astrologers in the daily and annual cycles embedded in our bodies. The timekeepers within us are linked to the magnetic environment at the time of our births. He hypothesises that the magnetic fields around all the planets resonate with our nervous systems in 'tunes' which we recognise. Each individual's tuning is determined by his or her genetic inheritance and we are each born when, as it were, the current pattern of planetary positions 'dials our number'. Our horoscopes are thus descriptions of what we are rather than – as is so often falsely understood – the causes of what we are. This accords with Rupert Sheldrake's theory of 'morphic resonance', and also with recently discovered medical evidence that it is hormonal changes in the foetus, not in the mother, that instigates the onset of labour. The metaphor, 'That rings a bell' thus takes on a newly significant connotation, as does our ascription to some people of a 'magnetic personality'.

But proving astrology experimentally is a difficult matter. Many correlations have been shown between people's psychological and physical characteristics and their natal horoscopes, and the horoscopes of parents and their children have commonalities overwhelmingly greater than occur by chance. But correlations are not proof. There are probably near-perfect correlations between having a stomach ulcer and drinking three or more cups of coffee a day, and being shortsighted and watching television for at least three hours a day. But these correlations do not prove that caffeine causes stomach ulcers nor that watching television causes shortsightedness.

In order to *prove* the existence of astrology as an independent factor, our experiments need to be designed so that significant positive results cannot be explained in any other way than that astrology is the *cause* of the results. Such experiments are difficult but not impossible to design. They need to be analogous to Pasteur's simply controlled, brilliant experiments which proved the existence of (then still invisible) microbes. Astrology, also, is presently 'invisible'.

The knowledge of a person that can be derived from a person's horoscope is deep and comprehensive. But the language of the horoscope is symbolic, and the quality of any interpretation is so dependent on the artistry and skill of the interpreter that it is extremely difficult to objectify the information.

Another significant problem in the design of any experiment to prove the validity of astrology is the need to control for the overwhelming importance of psychological factors. No experiments involving human responses can ever be entirely freed of the 'noise' of subjectivity, and unless the relevant psychological factors are maximally controlled, their noise will inevitably drown out the specific 'sound' we are striving to hear.

Bearing this in mind, in 1987, under the supervision of the late Professor Hans Eysenck, I designed and conducted an experiment to test the truth of astrology. I advertised for 'sceptical but open-minded' couples, married or in an intimate living-together relationship, and 122 respondents (61 couples) sent me their birth data. With the help of a computer programmer, on the basis of my interpretations of the astrological contacts ('synastry') between each couple, each individual was sent a description of how astrology saw them as experiencing their partner. Each individual was also sent four 'dummy' descriptions (based on other couples' astrological relationships). They were asked to rank the five descriptions from the most to the least true of their actual experience of their partner.

Forty-two respondents put the correct description in first place, and the overall results attested to the *existence of the astrological factor* at the 1% level of significance. (*Nature*, of course, refused to look at my experimental report.)

My own prediction is that by the end of this century we will have found in astrology the new blend of materialism and mystery, determinism and choice that we so crave. Astrology will become the generally accepted algebra that comprehensively encompasses our understanding of subject-matters as diverse as the genetic code, the physics of sub-atomic particles, the occurrence of natural catastrophes such as earthquakes and tidal waves, and the cycles of the stock market. And for those who care to do so, their appreciation of the transcendent nature of astrology will serve them in de-anthropomorphising God while retaining his superhuman awfulness, protection and will.

Life Stages

At every moment of our lives our overall response to our situation and to other people is informed by three contexts: the unchanging attributes of our humanity; our present stage of development in life; and our individuality. The relative influence of each of these contexts on a given moment may vary although, broadly speaking, our 'stage of development' tends to predominate in childhood and adolescence, our individuality in our middle years and, ideally, as we grow old, the spirituality associated with our humanity, especially in our coming to terms with aging and death.

In this essay I will describe the major stages of life depicted by the 'transits' of the planets Saturn, Uranus, Neptune, and Pluto to the same planets in our natal horoscopes. For the sake of those of my readers who are familiar with the astrological nature of the planets I will reference the particular planet participating in each of the stages. The orbit of Chiron (between Saturn and Uranus) is very erratic, so its transits to its natal place occur at different ages for different individuals, but I will interpret its universal return to its natal place at age 51. For the stages of childhood only I will include the Jupiter conjunction and opposition to its natal place as well as the (usually very noticeable!) first Mars return at about two years of age. I will also refer to the specific challenges facing all parents at particular stages of their child's development.

Irrespective of our individuality, we are all the same in being united in our lifelong concerns with pain and death, good versus evil, conflicting quests for excitement and security, and the overall quest for meaning in our lives. These are constant dynamic components of our minds that we need to be implicitly and explicitly aware of in every consideration of a horoscope of a human being.

Between our lifelong commonalities with all other human beings and the ultimate uniqueness of our individuality, there are stages of life that unite us in special ways with our near-contemporaries. It is often valuable and important to refer to these stages in consideration of the overall *meaning* of what a person is experiencing at any particular time.

These stages are additional to the transits that idiosyncratically and uniquely inform each individual's life.

It is also important to remember in reading the following interpretations that the particular manifestations of these universal life stages will be modified for each individual by delineations in his or her natal horoscope. For example, at his or her first Saturn return, somebody with natal Saturn in Gemini in the 7th house is likely to need to concentrate on issues of commitment in their intimate relationships, whereas somebody with natal Saturn in the 2nd house may need to concentrate on achieving financial security. Furthermore, natal aspects between Saturn and other planetary energies or sensitive points in the horoscope will also come into play. For example, somebody having natal Saturn trine Venus may experience their Saturn return as the time to get married, whereas somebody with natal Saturn square Midheaven may face redundancy or other difficulties in their career. Nonetheless, at age 28 to 30, all will, one way or another, experience a challenging and significant transition in their lives, as outlined in this essay.

Twenty-one months to two years. Mars conjunction Mars.

Until now the infant, however troublesome in other respects, has been essentially compliant (Please) to the Adapted Child constraints imposed on him, but now he makes it abundantly clear that he has an autonomous will. He turns his Please coin over and briefly expresses its defiant side as a preliminary to developing his Parent ego state. Assertive defiance and temper-tantrums are commonplace, and parents are now obliged to judge and decide their chosen approach to imposing civilising constraints on their child.

Five to Six. Jupiter opposition Jupiter and Saturn sextile Saturn

The typical five-year-old is a charming delight. The exuberance of Jupiter and the self-discipline of Saturn combine, and the child seems like a perfectly formed miniature adult, who now has a Parent ego state to complete his essential personality and character formation. Many children are just starting school at this age, the Jupiter opposition being manifest as great happy enthusiasm for what school teaches, and the Saturn sextile ensures that the child easily accommodates to the new restrictions imposed on him by the rules of the school. Now, for the first time, he begins to have to fend for himself, away from the protection of his mother, and this is also a significant and poignant moment for parents as they become fully conscious that healthy parenting means letting go of *their* dependence on their child's dependence on them. But, by and large, this is a stage of equilibrium and balance, and the child moves forward confidently to enlarge his world and achieve his goals without being difficult to control or being aggressively competitive with his peers. With his Parent ego state the child is now able appropriately sometimes to feel responsible or guilty and sometimes to righteously blame others. He is now capable of sharing and caring responses towards other people and expressing a considerable degree of self-discipline in maintaining his own general wellbeing. Now he understands the justifications for many of the Adapted Child prohibitions that were imposed on him when he was a toddler which, at that time, he was made non-comprehendingly simply to obey. Now he fears the retribution of his own conscience as much as the withdrawal of the approval of his mother and father.

He now knows that 'giving' as well as 'taking' is inevitably demanded of him if he is to receive the affectionate attention he wants from others. From now on, he is implicitly aware that *tenderness and aggression* have to be balanced in his or her desire for intimacy with others.

Seven Saturn square Saturn

At this time the child experiences her first 'identity crisis'. Insofar as the Saturn aspect is a square, it is an introverted crisis, more associated with the child's private awareness rather than to do with her relationships to other people. This is the time when the child first becomes aware of death in a realistic way and knows that everybody, including her mother and father and, most terrifyingly, she herself, will one day die. The fear of death is defended against by all human beings, and exaggeratedly so in childhood, from about this age onwards, with a markedly Be Perfect attitude to life that continues until puberty. Some children will openly express their terror of death, but for others it will be a closely guarded secret, observable only in the many compulsive rituals and magical rites they surround themselves with in their fearful bids to 'stop bad things happening' (the ultimate 'bad thing' being death) or in their inchoate fears of 'bogey men' or animals ... or any number of things. More defiantly, some children revel in war games, horror stories and violent films – the more gruesome, the better – although girls are more inclined to prefer psychological to physical viciousness.

However, these attitudes are only partly successful defences against the fear of death, which is the greatest threat to the child's confidence at this time. Cynicism and depression are more often experienced by a child during this stage of development than is commonly realised. Children are as capable of being depressed as adults, but are not articulate enough to describe the state as adults do. Prolonged quiet withdrawal from activities or from interactions with other people suggests a child may be depressed and in need of being *loved back to life* with abundant physical and verbal expressions of affection.

If parents themselves have a wholesomely positive attitude to life they need not fear that their seven-year-old's transient fears will be lasting. But however unspoken a child's fear of death is, parents need to be sensitive to it. If a child does express explicit fear of his or her own or others' deaths, in normal circumstances he should be told something along the lines of, 'Yes, everybody dies one day, but not until they are ready. Mummy and Daddy and you probably won't die for a very, very, very long time, until we've done all the things we want to.' Do not describe death as 'like going to sleep', which readily invokes in a child a fear of going to sleep; nor even as 'stopping breathing', which may prompt a child to fear that unless she self-consciously breathes she will die. Probably the best verbalisation for a child is some form of tautology like, 'You just stop being alive.'

When a grandparent or other loved old person dies, a child might be told, 'She was happy to die because she had had her turn of being alive and had done all the things she wanted to do. Of course it's sad for us that we won't see her again, but she can still make us happy when we remember her and talk about her.'

Subsidiarily, with the now dominant development of the Adult, Be Strong emotional detachment is characteristic of this stage of development between about seven and puberty. The child is less vulnerable now than she has been before or ever will be again in the face of emotional vicissitudes. (Sometimes, unhappily married parents decide they will stay together with their children until the children are adolescent, at which time, it is presumed, they will be better able to 'understand'. In fact, the adolescent is more emotionally vulnerable than at any other time of life, with the exception of the Oedipal stage of development between three and six. If needs must, a child is best able to cope with the separation of her parents if it takes place when she is between about six and twelve.)

Ten Saturn trine Saturn

This is a period of quiet equilibrium in the child before the storm of puberty. Children of this age have achieved a stable understanding of their own identity. All being well, by this time they have acquired basic numeracy and literacy, have become proficient in forming relationships with their peers, and usually have a same-sexed 'best friend'. They also feel pride in their status of being at the 'top' of their primary school.

Eleven to Twelve Jupiter conjunction Jupiter

As the first Jupiter cycle in the life is completed and added to the equilibrium and self-control of the Saturn trine Saturn transit at age ten, at age eleven to twelve the child's calm and confident commonsensical attitude to life reaches its peak, and he looks forward to the excitement of starting secondary school. The new Jupiter cycle represents a new cycle of growth and progress in the child's education and increased freedom through acquired competencies. He or she experiences and enjoys new privileges, like staying up later in the evenings, perhaps being allowed for the first time to ride his bicycle to school, increased pocket money, etc. If this is their first child, parents may feel that their essential task of parenting is accomplished and they are proud of themselves and their child for the disciplined, sensible, considerate young person he or she has become. Little do they know!

Fourteen to Fifteen Saturn opposition Saturn and Uranus sextile Uranus

Almost overnight the calm, controlled, sensible, considerate, Be Perfect child becomes the seething cauldron of Hurry Up hormones, often displaying wild mood swings associated with all the excitement of becoming fully sexually aware (Uranus) and the reality (Saturn) that the world and parents and teachers will not allow them the fulfilment of all their impulses. Virtually all his Adult and Parent are suppressed, and his manifest personality is essentially composed of libidinous and aggressive Free Child and rebellious Adapted Child. The Saturn and Uranus transits of this time are amongst the most disturbing combination that most people experience in their lives (although a similar crisis arises around thirty-eight to forty-two). Whereas the first crisis of confidence accompanying the Saturn square at age seven was an introspective one, demanding new ways of coping with the self in the face of mortality, the Saturn opposition finds expression as an extraverted first poignant awareness that other people exert power and control over us against our own will. Combined with the Uranus sextile, the typical response to the coercion of parents and teachers and the restrictions of the world-in-general is at least protest if not outright rebellion. There is probably only one more disturbing state of being than being a fourteen-to-fifteen-year-old and that is being the parent of one! However, parents can find comfort in the fact that their moody and difficult pubescent child is perfectly normal, although they are now challenged to rise to their highest level of parenting skills.

Seventeen to Nineteen Jupiter opposition Jupiter and Saturn trine Saturn

These Jupiter and Saturn transits declare that 'the worst is over' for the adolescent – and his or her parents! The child is beginning again to be both exuberantly enthusiastic about life and appropriately self-disciplined and considerate of other people – the child last seen, fleetingly, at the combined Jupiter and Saturn transits when he or she was between five and six years old. The young adult now has probably achieved some educational qualifications and is preparing, calmly and with control, to look forward to further education and the willing acceptance of adult responsibilities. But the final stage of moral maturity is still to be achieved. At this stage the child knows that she still needs her parents to help her consolidate all their moral teachings in her Parent and, in this respect, she continues to challenge them.

This is a markedly Try Hard, competitive stage of development. Phenomenally, the adolescent wants to defeat her parents' moral exhortations, which she challenges with her now sophisticated Adult; but she is actually playing a game. Covertly, she is begging her parents to show the stalwartness of their Parent convictions so that she, the child, can interject their values in readiness for going out into the world and managing away from home. When parents see through the child's specious games and firmly insist on the validity of their values, the child is deeply grateful – although she is unlikely to say so, at least until she is confidently established in the grown-up world and maybe not until she is a parent herself.

Twenty-one to Twenty-two Saturn square Saturn and Uranus square Uranus

Now the young adult steps out into grown-up life and makes his or her first autonomous choice to 'do his thing', sow his wild oats and live for present impulse (Uranus); or to work hard to establish himself securely within the conventional structures of society (Saturn). While the choice may not be a complete either-or, by and large one of these alternatives is chosen and the other put aside.

Twenty-two to Twenty-five. Jupiter conjunction Jupiter and Saturn sextile Saturn

Another combination of Jupiter and Saturn transits mark a further development of the now young adult's sensible, controlled and enthusiastic embarkation on a new cycle of learning and assumption of adult responsibilities.

This is the time when, in most developed cultures, the child completes the gradual process of leaving his parents' home. The emotional process of making the radical detachment from parents associated with no longer living with them usually takes a few years to complete. In many societies, at about age eighteen children begin their tertiary education in places other than their home-town, which is a useful external structure students are granted that enables them to have left home during term-time and yet to return home during vacations in a natural way that avoids any loss of face for them. Then by about age twenty-two the child should be capable of making the final severance of his attachment to his parents' home and creating his own domestic environment.

Twenty-seven to Thirty. Saturn conjunction Saturn, Uranus trine Uranus, Neptune sextile Neptune.

This is a time of reckoning and one of the most significant turning points in life. True adulthood begins now as the individual realises the world is not his oyster, but rather that his life is severely circumscribed by his abilities, his childhood conditioning and the consequences of the choices he has already made. Depression is common at this time, accompanied by a feeling of, 'My life is nearly half over and I've accomplished nothing!' In truth, the life of the autonomous self is just beginning. Those who rebelled against staid conventionality at twenty-one now urgently want to 'settle down'; those who created conventional structures in their lives may feel desperate to escape from the prisons they feel they have locked themselves in. Childhood is over; adulthood begins with the realisation that only we can make our dreams come true by what we are willing to do and to be responsible for ourselves.

Thirty-four. Saturn sextile Saturn

As at twenty-four to twenty-five, a time of equilibrium and balance as conscious goals are pursued.

Thirty-five to Thirty-six. Saturn square Saturn

Between the crucial awareness associated with the first Saturn return at twenty-eight to thirty and the mid-thirties most young adults are progressively and diligently pursuing their personal goals. But at thirty-five to thirty-six stumbling blocks are encountered and/or a sense of boredom and stagnation sets in. Early ambitions for affluence and prestige may be well on their way to fulfilment, but the price now seems high. Life seems full of duty and responsibility.

Thirty-eight to Forty-four. Saturn opposition Saturn, Uranus opposition Uranus, Neptune square Neptune and (for recent generations) Pluto square Pluto

Between thirty-eight and forty-four life crises crowd in on one another and the individual may wonder if he will ever again be free of depression, self-doubt, onerous burdens and obligations, nervous instability, confusion about anything and everything, painful confrontations and forced catharses of his deepest hang-ups. This is a time of reckoning for choices made, and past personal goals are now see as illusory in terms of their hoped for satisfactions.

But concurrently there is excitement, albeit unstable and somewhat frightening, for this is also a time of revelation, when the mind is opened to new possibilities and, for the first time, the 'other side' of some coin we have been trading with all our lives is seen. Long-buried ambitions, often dating back to the dreams of glory we had for ourselves at our first Saturn opposition when we were fourteen or fifteen, may resurface and seek fulfilment. At first, in response to the excitement of this time, the individual may kick over the traces of whatever area of life his new awareness pertains to, and the 'opposite' values of the past may be totally discarded. However, gradually, the new and the old are recognised as two sides of one coin and they become integrated at a higher level where they are no longer incompatible.

Forty-seven to Forty-eight. Saturn trine Saturn

A period of steady and responsible work within the established structures of the individual's life, giving satisfaction and a sense of security.

Forty-nine to Fifty-one. Saturn square Saturn and Chiron conjunction Chiron.

The individual has no option now but to admit he or she is middle-aged, and there is a last surge of ambitious energy directed to the fulfilment of personal ambitions 'before it is too late'. Concurrently, especially for those people who are conscious of bearing deep scars from their childhood wounds, there is a dissolution of fears lived with up until now, and a serene self-acceptance begins to emerge.

Fifty-three to Fifty-four. Saturn sextile Saturn

Personal challenges that were met at forty-nine to fifty-one are now integrated as achieved structures in life, and opportunities open up for new patterns of living. For many people this is associated with the last of their children leaving home.

Fifty-six to Sixty. Saturn conjunction Saturn, Uranus trine Uranus and Neptune trine Neptune

This time is in many ways a recapitulation of the 'identity crisis' of twenty-eight to thirty. We are again forced to face our limitations and we again feel that 'time is running out'. As twenty-eight to thirty brought awareness of the limitations of our abilities and our childhood conditioning as a preliminary to autonomously pursuing our self-development, fifty-six to sixty brings awareness of how far we have fulfilled our worldly ambitions and recognition that the era of achievement in the wider world is nearly over. Now we should have, and appropriately want, more time to enjoy contemplative pursuits, general relaxation, and the enjoyment of life for its own sake. While we may not be able from now on to gain much more power in the external world, this is compensated for by our realisation that we now care more for self-approval than for the world's evaluation of us. We are looking forward to progressive changes in our lives arising from our diminished need for striving, and we are becoming more idealistic and serene.

Sixty to Sixty-three Uranus square Uranus, Saturn sextile Saturn

For many people retirement is looming or has already begun. Now is the time to create new structures in our lives and to have adventures of mind and/or body that our past responsibilities have curtailed.

Sixty-five to Sixty-six Saturn square Saturn

For those who took the opportunity of their Uranus square Saturn sextile between sixty and sixty-three, this will be a time of consolidation of new structures in the life. For those who are unprepared, old age may loom only as sad renunciation.

Sixty-seven. Saturn trine Saturn. As for previous Saturn trine Saturn transits, a period of equilibrium.

Sixty-nine to Seventy-two. Saturn opposition Saturn and Uranus sextile Uranus.

This is a recapitulation of the same transits when we were fourteen to fifteen. Now we know that our 'three-score-years-and-ten' are up, and continued life is a bonus. Now is the time when we need to put our worldly affairs in order in readiness for death. But at the same time there is also a sense that our duties are finished and, with whatever life is left to us, we are entitled to 'do our own thing', out of which a seventy-year-old may develop a new enthusiasm or activity or new friendships, untrammelled by any 'oughts'.

Seventy-seven Saturn trine Saturn. As for the same transit at previous stages, a time for productive consolidation of established structures in the life.

Eighty. Saturn square Saturn. We can no longer avoid the realisation that we are old and need to accept the limitations that our age imposes on us.

Eighty-two. Saturn sextile Saturn. As for previous Saturn sextile Saturn transits.

Eighty-four to Eighty-Nine and Beyond. Saturn conjunction Saturn, Uranus conjunction Uranus, Neptune opposition Neptune.

For the many people who now achieve this age we might say it is 'the new three-score-years-and-ten', to which the obituary columns bear witness. For those who have fulfilled the potential of their horoscopes and have reached this era, it is a time of wisdom and detachment. Ideally, with a holistic sense of 'mission accomplished', we withdraw from mundane concerns into a serene mystical transcendence of the self and all its fears and strivings and a calm readiness to die.

Zeitgeist

Our deepest concerns – love, death, meaning, fate and free-will – seem to be timeless and immutable. But we are so constituted as to keep wondering and struggling to find better ways of understanding ourselves than have so far been achieved. In the parlance of today, this quest may be seen as a reflection of our homeostatic disposition, the constant pull-push of arousal and quiescence that is written into our biology and which has amongst its spin-offs all of art, science and philosophy.

Probably the longest cycle in the history of ideas is the alternating orientations of holism and atomism. Although neither orientation has ever been entirely absent, the general tenor of human thought seems to have begun holistic and then started swinging towards atomistic about two and a half thousand years ago, apparently reaching its apogee in the twentieth century, from which time it has begun to turn. Physics seems to have reached the turning point first, expressed in Heisenberg's uncertainty principle and Einstein's theory of relativity, but biology is still engaged in the triumphalism of the human genome and atomistic brain research. And psychology, which only began to be atomistic when most other fields of endeavour were nearly finished with analysis, as an academic discipline is wildly out of step with the current zeitgeist.

Outside academia, psychology seems to have found its contemporary voice by blending itself with philosophy and medicine, both of which fields have branches that seem precisely to reflect the compromises between materialism and mystery, determinism and choice which characterise humanity's present hovering outlook. In philosophy, existentialism is the name of the game, in medicine it is homeopathy. Some current epigenetic research suggests that our evolution as a species has been accelerated even to the extent of permanent changes now being visibly transmitted from one generation to the next. (Or is it the Lamarckian hypothesis coming into its own again?) Certainly it seems that just lately our left-brains have achieved parity with our right-brains and we are embarking on an era of right-and left-brain synthesis that is called New Age thinking.

But the mundane reality of people's professional lives has lagged behind the movement of theories. The twentieth century was still one of increasing specialization in which people were required to know more and more about less and less in order to procure their PhDs and ensure their viability in the employment marketplace. In many subjects, knowledge continued to be particularised to its limits; and perhaps most importantly for the general human condition, academics and others became more and more unhappily isolated in the autism of their specialisations. Only in the past few years has there been a burgeoning of inter-disciplinary conferences and cogent but popular writing about science that extends communication and nourishing strokes for intellectual givers and receivers alike.

It is no longer infra dig for academics to step outside their ivory towers and communicate simply with the intelligent lay public. Not only has this represented a backlash against the loneliness of those whose expertise is ultra-specialised; it is also a manifestation of a contemporary cultural climate in which academia is called upon to justify the funds it receives, and academic salaries are relatively low. Books such as James Gleich's *Chaos* (1988), John Gray's *Straw Dogs* (2002) and Dava Sobell's *Longitude* (2007), as well as many science-made-easy television programmes have flourished, and such authors and television presenters are now envied rather than disdained by their colleagues for their popular acclaim and monetary gain.

While the particular pre-occupations of any age may be seen with hindsight to be transient or even trivial, to the people alive at a given time they are imperatively demanding of attention. Though I am conscious of the unavoidable blinkeredness of my own here-and-now perspective, I believe there are a number of contemporary conditions that are stretching our innate adaptability to critical limits.

By far the biggest change in human consciousness over the past fifty years has been the emergence of universal awareness of the world's population explosion. It is estimated that about six percent of all the human beings who have ever lived are alive today. Our awareness of this critical situation was not the case even in the 1950s. Especially in Australia, where I was then living, there was plenty of room for everybody, full employment, and government hoardings that exhorted us to 'populate or perish'. Our individual existences were valued and useful to the collective, we knew we were needed and so were full of buoyant self-esteem.

Now, we all know there are far too many of us and the world could well do without us individually. Collectively, self-esteem is low, especially among the working classes whose unskilled labour has greatly diminished in value. In the developed countries with which we are familiar the contented, conservative, reliable, conscientious working class personality, full of pride and dignity, has been replaced by a personality type that is envious, bitter, pugnacious, amoral, hostile and despairing. As a species, we have become like rats in an overcrowded cage; and interactive internet sites – Facebook, Twitter, Tweet ... seem to represent a flailing bid people are making to reassert their individual importance in the world at large.

The most extreme outcome of this critically unstable scenario is that, one way or another, like countless other species, we will fail to rise to the challenge and will become extinct. Yet there is already a spontaneous corrective response to our crisis of overpopulation that suggests we may save ourselves. Notwithstanding the desperate bids of many infertile couples to overcome their infertility with the aid of science, there are now many people – and especially women – who are voluntarily renouncing parenthood out of their own free-will. This was virtually unheard of when I was first married fifty years ago when having babies was the unreflective desire of all couples; and the small proportion of infertile couples would almost surely adopt the surplus of unwanted births as quickly as possible. Although the rise in declared homosexuality in some developed countries is clearly associated with its decriminalisation, it may be that its rise is factual as well as apparent, that is, an unconscious collective response to the world's population crisis. And the proscription in China against having more than one child certainly suggests that a species-preservative adaptation is under way. Even the use of 'weapons of mass destruction' may have an ecological purpose. Only time will tell; but we are meanwhile faced with the here-and-now reality of many individuals with deeply undermined self-esteem associated with their perception of their personal redundancy. This is a primary contemporary contingency of the human condition.

The diminishment of individual self-esteem in our over-populated world has also had a kind of compensatory backlash in the form of self-centred opportunism and an angry rejection of authority.

A hundred years ago, in the absence of antibiotics and central heating, life was shorter and physically much more uncomfortable than today. Nevertheless, self-sufficiency was for most people possible most of the time; whereas today the sophisticated demands we have for our health, comfort and amusement feel like survival needs, and we are ever more dependent on others to provide and maintain what have become essentials in our lives.

Thus was born professionalism, which is nurturing, reassuring know-how. We are all professionals now, each purveying some small Parent ego state expertise in response to the ever-expanding imperative Child needs that only others can satisfy. Implicit in nearly every payment we now make to another is the agitated cry, 'I'm helpless, make it better for me', from the TV repair man, to our personal trainers, gym instructors, hairdressers, plastic surgeons and financial advisers. Survival is ever more psychological and feels ever more frighteningly tenuous.

A hundred years ago there were few professions and the professions there were – doctors, lawyers, teachers, and the clergy – were revered and trusted for their unquestionable (Parent) integrity and selfless concern for the people they served. Now, professionalism is democratised to include multitudes whose orientation is me-first (Child) rather that you-first (Parent), so we feel justified in *mis*trusting the plethora of servants we rely on to keep our cars, televisions, computers, plumbing and roofs in states of repair; and we also call to account. Constant invigilation insults professional autonomy; complaints procedures abound, professionals who touch those in their care risk being charged with criminal abuse, targets are set for teachers and doctors as if they were manufacturers of consumables. Teachers used to be able to count on the explicit endorsement of their authority by the parents of their pupils; now they are often abused and sometimes even physically attacked by some parents as well as children. Patients used to trust and revere the care and expertise of their doctors; now they sue them at the drop of a stethoscope.

Now the frightened Child in us all escalates its rebellious tyranny in the name of freedom while actually desperately seeking the containment of a confidently and lovingly controlling Parent. And the deposed Parent, divested of authority and respect, resorts to indemnity policies against litigation, or else bows out completely. At the time of writing (January 2012), according to a recent survey, a third of teachers say they want to leave their profession within the next five years, and a quarter of doctors want to quit their jobs. In America, in some high-risk areas of medical practice like neurosurgery, doctors are choosing to retire early rather than pay malpractice insurance premiums of up to $200,000 per annum.

Undoubtedly there are abuses of Parental power – in the home and in society at large – that need to be addressed and dealt with by any civilised society; and maybe our present Zeitgeist in this regard is an appropriate swing of the pendulum against such abuses in previous generations. Nevertheless, it seems that our contemporary overload of politically correct and health-and-safety proscriptions is an extreme that both reflects and reinforces the profound existential dis-ease that is the hallmark of our time.

Derivative from the suspicions and general mistrust that are accorded professionals today, so too are parents and adults in general disrespected by children. In their authority over their children, parents have no choice but to do battle with media-inculcated competitive materialism, moral relativity, and precocious sexuality. And parents feel obliged to impose on themselves frenzied and expensive bids to gain places for their children in schools that will give them the best chances for attaining a high place in the pecking order of life.

It used to be the case that children stayed innocent of greedy materialism until their teenage years when their desire for fashionable clothes and other possessions bears witness to their burgeoning need for sexual display. But in response to the market forces of capitalism, communicated to children principally through television advertising, over the past forty or fifty years children have become 'consumers' and 'customers' at ever earlier ages, their innocence ruthlessly exploited by canny manufacturers of 'must-haves' for every tiny tot. Birthday parties can no longer be simple celebrations, but every one competitively elaborate and expensive.

In the face of these forces, the most puritanical of parents find it virtually impossible to deprive their children of the goods that 'everybody' has; and those parents who, by dint of poverty, are unable to provide these goods know the cruel scorn and humiliation their children will experience in the playground.

And rarely is it possible today for the income of one parent to suffice for a family's needs. Most mothers are obliged to have at least part-time paid employment to meet the enormous cost of paying the mortgage, which is the average family's anxious obsession.

Until about thirty years ago, when they were not at school, children 'went out to play', freely adventuring with other children who lived nearby. Typically, children left the house soon after breakfast, sometimes returning briefly for lunch but often taking picnic supplies with them and only returning home in the late afternoon. They lived in the wonderland of imaginative play and the invigorating largesse of physical exploration of the outdoor environment. And the vast majority of children walked or cycled to school on their own, wrapped in the privacy of their autonomous selfhood.

Now, in the name of both safety and practicality, children are rarely separated from their parents, and both parents and children – whose activities and conversations are naturally so often boring to each other – are bound, often for hours every day, to be locked together in the confines of a car, in mutual irritation and frustrated freedom, as the children are fetched and carried to school, to distant friends and to attendance at the numerous activities by which their days are programmed. For parents and children, respite from each other's company tends to be limited to the hours children plonk themselves in front of computers or television, locked in couch-potato virtual reality. Despite all our domestic machinery, designed for human ease and comfort, daily life is enormously more confined and anxious than it used to be.

We now live in a Child-led rather than a Parent-led culture. Until about forty years ago children, generally without prompting, surrendered their seats on buses or elsewhere to adults; now, many don't do so even for the obviously old or frail. Teachers could count on the explicit endorsement of their authority by the parents of their pupils; now they are often abused and attacked by some parents as well as children. Moral relativity is politically *de rigueur*. Adults are no longer consensually united in their moral values and codes of behaviour, leaving children – and the Child in all of us – anxiously bereft of the security of authoritative containment.

Today we are free to be monogamous or polygamous, heterosexual, bisexual or homosexual, single or joint parents, and all these options are displayed and purveyed through the devices of capitalism as available commodities. Notwithstanding that most adults, through their deeper instinctual and experiential wisdom, abjure the despair and nihilism associated with untrammelled sexual licence, children are constantly bombarded with 'the facts', which they can only cope with through precocious and specious awareness.

First five-year-old: Guess what I found on our patio this morning? A used condom.

Second five-year-old: What's a patio?

As witnesses to their parents' serial bed partners, multitudes of children are burdened with the primal anxiety associated with explicitly knowing the manifest reality of their parents' sexual behaviour. And there are few parents left who have the conviction or the courage to exhort their teenage children to pre-marital chastity in the name of idealism. Aids has become the only warning deterrent against free-and-easy sexual behaviour.

Notwithstanding that by the beginning of the twentieth century the constraints of religious observance were rapidly declining in favour of passionate devotion to the freedoms made available by science and technology, habit died hard, and most people, however perfunctorily, regularly and dutifully attended places of worship. So too was secular daily life contained in the obsessively ritualistic timetabling of washing, ironing, cleaning, baking, visiting relatives, going for drives in the country ... and most people ate fish on Fridays, roast beef and Yorkshire pudding on Sundays, and a very limited range of meals on other days of the week as well. Until the 1960s life was ritualised to an extent almost unbelievable to those too young to remember. The absence of choice bound everything in place through ceremony and continuity.

Present-day secular existentialism burdens us with choice. Not only are we free shamelessly to be and do as we please in secular matters, but in virtually every other aspect of our lives as well. We are free to eat at home or on the street at any time, to work sixteen hours a day or beg in the subway. Virtually all observance – religious or secular – has been dissolved in favour of the freedom and addictive delights attendant on our affluence. The only taboo against freedom of self-expression is of opinion, which we call political correctness.

When Paris dictated the length of our hemlines, when we were not allowed to leave the table until everybody had finished, when children called all familiar but unrelated adults 'auntie' or 'uncle', when strawberries in August were a treat, when couples – at least nominally – refrained from full sexual congress until they were married, and we were generally obliged to conform to the consensually agreed values and constraints of society as a whole, we hid our deviances in willing hypocrisy (hypocrisy being the homage that vice pays to virtue). Thus we were free to concentrate on things that really mattered to us as individuals, unencumbered by the numbing demand of forever having to choose.

Contemporary individualistic freedom, reinforced by material abundance, cruelly demands of the two-year-old in each of us,

'Vanilla, chocolate, or strawberry?' A friend of mine who is a market researcher tells me it has been found that most jams and marmalades are sold by manufacturers who offer up to four – but no more – varieties.

Our pleasures are contained in the transitional moment of quiescence consequent on the satiation of desire, before the memory of desire is quite faded and before the movement that is called being alive propels us to chase after another desire. Desire seeks its fulfilment in pleasure, but pleasure is not guaranteed. Intrinsic to the process is the risk of failure and an associated degree of pain proportional to the pleasure sought. Maximum pleasure for extraverts is associated with relatively large amounts of arousing stimulation; maximum pleasure for introverts is associated with relatively large amounts of quiescence.

Until lately in human history one of the chief balancers of speed, excitement and adventure in our lives was the predictability, order and safety of religion, its proscriptions and its prescribed rituals. Pilgrimages and holy wars provided participants with a satisfying blend of dangerous excitement and safe discipline through the life-risking dangers of travel and war and the immutable conviction of righteous certainty in the name of God's will and protection. The latter-day equivalent is travelling in the name of Work, with lower levels of both commitment and excitement than en route to a Crusade, but with a fair homeostatic balance maintained.

With or without benefit of an obsessively informed mission, travelling is a universally and timelessly popular means of satisfying our episodic needs for stepping outside the safe, established structure of our lives into speedy excitement. But implicit in the promises of travel is that the planning and effort we invest in the process is proportional to the pleasurable excitement of adventure and novelty that we achieve.

Before the invention of the steam engine and the bicycle the greatest attainable speed for human beings was that of a horse, and the best possible comfort and safety was found in a closed vehicle pulled by a horse over roads incomparably bumpier than our present-day worst. But a few miles of travel could reward us with a novelty value – changed culture, changed dialect – that we now have to travel long distances to achieve. Now speed of communication and transport has effectively fulfilled Marshall McLuhan's prophecy fifty years ago that the world would become a global village.

As well as the increased speed (and decreased novelty) with which we are now able to move our bodies, we also have telephones, faxes, mobile phones, email, the internet ... designed primarily to give us forms of communication previously undreamt of. They also, incidentally, add ever-increasing speed to every facility they provide us with. So speed has become an addiction in our lives, a substance – like cigarettes or drugs – whose ingestion we are persuaded is the means of satisfying our appetite for time, but provides only fleeting illusions of time gained while creating an ever-increasing craving for it. In the developed world – and in the aspirations of the rest of the world – money is abundant and time very scarce.

While much of our contemporary addiction to actual speed can be attributed to the speed that is intrinsically valued in the products of technology, some of it is also a compensation for the diminishment of excitement (which is biologically the equivalent of speed) inherent in the novelties of the changing seasons.

Central heating and air-conditioning make our lives optimally physically comfortable throughout the year; we are continuously offered a super-abundance of foods from around the world; and our gluttonous appetite for television cookery programmes testifies to our need for ever more sophisticated novelty in our daily food to compensate for the no longer existent pleasures of seasonally limited delicacies like strawberries and asparagus, and the novelties of previously untried foods when we travelled abroad. Now, at home and abroad, high streets are swamped by multi-national chains purveying identical goods. And even the most challenging physical adventures like climbing Mount Everest have been made almost safe, easy and commonplace.

Fast food, fast cars, fast sex, fast money, fast divorce, and fast celebrity are the order of the day. The Far East and the Antipodes have become *de rigueur* minimum requirements for European youth in search of their adventures; and we are fast running out of novel possibilities on earth – witness the recent space tourist who paid £14,000,000 for the exclusively better, more distant and more exciting adventure of accompanying two astronauts on their scientific mission.

So speed and busyness dominate our lives, our diaries being fuller into the more and more distant future. Addictively, we grasp for time in our specious bid to overcome the anxiety that our technological time-savers have created. The integrity of our nervous systems is at stake.

Ironically, obsessive religious fundamentalism is one form of homeostatic backlash against the excesses of danger and speed. But suicide bombing represents the implosion of speed and compulsiveness at the limit of both. Too much arousal leads to danger which, in extremis, leads to death; perfect stillness *is* death. More gently, there is continuing growth in the popularity of quiescent activities such as transcendental meditation and yoga, the self-discipline of perfecting our bodies at the gym, and obsessiveness about maintaining our health and fitness and prolonging our lives through diet and dietary supplements. Self-regulation of our homeostatic need to balance exciting speed and calm self-discipline is beginning to gain ground again at life-enhancing levels of oppositeness and tension between them.

We live in interesting times!

The Life and Death of God

Out of the buzzing, whirring, inchoate oneness into which we are thrust as new-born babies, the first separated 'facts' we apprehend are our bodily experiences of contentment versus pain. We like contentment; we don't like pain. In due course this basic dichotomy gets refined by further differentiation, and we become able to name and to calibrate our experiences as different kinds and degrees of contentment and pain. We continually struggle to maintain contentment and eliminate pain from our lives, but we never succeed for long. So the first truth we seek in our lives is that which makes sense of these two facts – contentment and pain. Contentment becomes 'good' and pain becomes 'bad'.

Soon we come to realise that our attempts to eliminate pain from our lives are essentially and repeatedly doomed to failure, and this realisation becomes another fact that needs to be made sense of in our hard-wired quest to understand our experiences. So the second essential theory we formulate invariably construes 'good' and 'evil' forces that permeate the universe. And the unavoidable corollary to this truth is that, inasmuch as we ourselves are part and parcel of the universe, the good and evil forces of the universe must also be in us. Notwithstanding the very great variations in belief systems of different cultures, no culture can manage life without the concepts of 'good and evil' and their immediate offshoots, 'blame and guilt' and 'reward and punishment'. These concepts are the necessary foundation for all our individual and collective meanings of life, which our minds need in order to rationalise the pain in our lives.

We begin life without any awareness of the separateness of ourselves from the universe. But from when we first say 'I' we become more and more consciously differentiated from everybody else; we develop our self-esteem, our egos. Our self-esteem, by rights, should grow and grow until, fully assured of our individual worth, we begin to transcend our egos and, ideally, come full circle to oneness with the universe again, as achieved by the mystic.

The task of developing our egos is essentially the task of struggling through our fears – our hang-ups – which, in the final analysis may be reduced to our fear of death. Knowledge of our mortality is the central, universal pain of life, although each of us, in accordance with the individual differences between people, has specific fears and associated pains that we struggle to overcome. The struggle for a well-developed ego – a sense of our own importance through our achievements – is a manifestation of our doomed-to-fail quest for immortality.

But essentially futile as it is, this battle must be fought and won, though the war must inevitably be lost. The happinesses that are available to us in our limited lives are contingent on our living life *as if* it has meaning – even if it doesn't. While we are experiencing pain, intrinsically 'it doesn't make sense', so unless we have faith that meaning is contained in it (even though we don't presently know that meaning) we will translate our feeling that we are experiencing something 'senseless' into a bitter and nihilistic attitude to life itself. Faith that there is wisdom greater than our own in God (or the powers-that-be) is needed for us to interpret our pains as having a *purpose* (however presently unknown) that is furthering our long-term happiness. We confirm this when we retrospectively interpret our past pains as having brought us knowledge, without which we would not be able fully to appreciate our present joys and achieved sense of meaning in our lives.

Thus armed with our basic category of 'good and evil', with evil as the definitive 'cause' of pain and death, we naturally seek to *be good* and thereby avoid pain and death. But we certainly can't avoid death, and although, in multitudinous ways, we do learn to attribute to our own 'goodness' the avoidance of quotidian pains, and it 'serves us right' if we put our hands in fire and are burnt, Job in all of us is forced to acknowledge that there is an incomprehensible gap in the perfect correspondence we would like to see between goodness and reward and evil and punishment. We do avoid the pain of being burnt by being 'good' and not touching hot stoves; but a completely unpredicted gas explosion may set fire to our house and us. We avoid being arrested and sent to gaol by being 'good' and law-abiding; but Nazis can come and round us up and throw us into concentration camps. Love given is usually reciprocated; but sometimes love is responded to with a spit in the eye. Being 'good' by eating a healthy diet and exercising does tend to protect and prolong our lives and free us from illness and pain; but the young and 'innocent' may be smitten with cruel and mortal illnesses while the 'bad' live long and healthy lives.

If goodness was never rewarded and badness was never punished we would happily become moral nihilists. If goodness was always rewarded and badness always punished, we would have no need of moral debate. But the reality in which we live is that goodness is *usually* rewarded and badness is *usually* punished.

We are left with the tantalising ambiguity that pains, both physical and psychological, can demonstrably be shown to be at least delayed by our 'goodness' – except when they are not! And this conundrum leads inevitably to the second basic construct of the human mind: 'fate versus free-will'. In the name of fate, we inevitably invent God, who becomes the Final Cause that determines both our inescapable mortality and the painful contingencies of our lives that we are unable to connect to our own causative 'badness'. Thus, by intermittent reinforcement – the most powerful of all conditioning techniques – God tantalises us into forever questing to understand His will.

'The problem of free-will' daunts us. It cannot be solved, only dis-solved. The existence or non-existence of 'meaning' and 'fate' are concepts that refer to a 'higher' state of consciousness than our own. An insect on the receiving end of the 'free-will' of my foot in crushing it is experiencing its fate when the incident is interpreted simply in terms of my power over it. More complexly, wasn't the insect responsible for not seeing my foot and avoiding it? And even more complexly, from the insect's point of view, if I (whose power is infinitely greater than its) have chosen to crush it under my foot, why did I choose to do so? Maybe for the obvious (to it) sin it committed against me by stinging me. But maybe it didn't sting me and didn't even try, and in its dying moment it rages against me for my 'injustice'. (Think of all the insects who do sting people and get away with it!) Did I kill it punitively in accordance with a morality of my own outside its ken? From a 'superior' position in order to demonstrate its 'nothingness' to me? Because I am intrinsically 'evil'? It could never know. It – and we – can only solve the problem by living at the highest level of free-will available to our consciousness, while accepting (from the evidence) that there are bound to be times in our lives when a bigger consciousness than we are capable of mocks our morality and conscious purposes. It is simply pragmatically the case that we live our lives most satis-factorily (to ourselves) when we behave *as if* our free-will is paramount. As an unknown rabbi succinctly put it, 'We've got to believe in free-will, we've got no choice.'

So in those occurrences in all our lives when even our own unconscious motives cannot be seen to account for what befalls us, we are reduced to impotent acquiescence to Fate, that is God's Will. All that is left for us to decide is whether, on balance, the universe is basically a friendly or an unfriendly place, whether 'good' outweighs 'evil', whether God himself is essentially benevolent or essentially malevolent. To the extent that we perceive good to be the pervasive dominating force in the universe, we see ourselves as predominantly 'good'; to the extent that we perceive evil to be the pervasive dominating force in the universe, we see ourselves as predominantly 'evil'.

Happiness is not guaranteed to those who perceive the universe to be, on balance, 'good', but *un*happiness is demonstrably inevitable for those who perceive the universe to be, on balance, 'evil'. Thus religions, which all contain the assumption that God and the universe are, on balance, good, represent the accumulated wisdom of mankind concerning how we can live most contentedly in the face of our contingent pains and the overwhelming pain of our knowledge of our mortality.

Free-will is maintained in the quality of our responses to our fate – basically whether, as Jung put it, 'we do gladly that which we must', or stamp at our fate with impotent rage. The religious orientation is to go willingly, however uncomprehendingly, with whatever fate metes out to us, the reward for which is the eventual beatitude of the mystic for whom even the fear of death is transcended and for whom everything is neither good nor bad, simply the way things are. Ironically, this hard-won perspective of the mystic is the way of being for other species, who, without intermediary cogitation, simply live their lives 'for no reason', in accordance with the biological propellants of their constitutions. But then other species do not have an anticipatory fear of death to overcome!

For those of us who have not yet achieved the detached beatitude of the mystic, theologians seek to convince us that, no matter how we suffer, ultimately everything is for the best in this, the best of all possible universes. Indeed, they are often inclined to argue that pain and suffering are privileges implying future rewards not to be granted to those who do not suffer. All that we see is the meaningless tangle of threads on the back of the tapestry; only God sees the beautiful coherent picture on the front.

But contemporarily we have reached a critical turning point in our relationship to God, the culmination of about 500 years of increasing dissatisfaction with ourselves, and therefore with Him, because whether we theistically believe we are made in God's image or atheistically believe God is made in our image, we and He are very alike. As Pascal put it, 'If triangles had a god he would have three sides.'

Copernicus demoted us from being the centre of the universe, Darwin humbled us into realising that we are not special among species, and Freud clinched our humiliation by insisting we don't even know our own minds. At first, God fought back valiantly, bringing down his wrath on hubristic man in the form of the Black Death and sundry other collective calamities, and on particular men and women in the form of inquisitions, burnings and derision. But by the beginning of the twentieth century the theories of science could confidently account for the most horrendous acts of God in materialistic terms. We cannot pretend not to know what we do know, so we and God have thus been reduced to puny impotence. As a consequence, for the first time in human history, for very many people God has been pronounced dead.

Yet mankind's new-found collective willingness to challenge the existence of God has not obviated our need to give meaning to our lives, and the twentieth century sought to replace the reassuring certainty of God's existence with the reassurance of Science. But the implications of Heisenberg's uncertainty principle, Einstein's theory of relativity, and post-Einsteinian cosmologies full of *un*certainties and such nihilistic horrors as Black Holes and Chaos theory have permeated the everyday existential consciousness of very large number of people. Without God to fall back on we are left trembling at Nothing, struggling to outstare the emptiness of a godless universe. Stripped of our centrality in the universe, stripped of our specialness amongst species, stripped of the hegemony of our conscious minds, we have no choice, if we are to resurrect God, but to fully de-anthropomorphise him.

Contemporary 'humanism' claims for itself the ability to educate our young and pursue our lives morally, with rationality and without any need for God. I believe this is illusory. We are overwhelmingly *irrational;* our (Parent) beliefs – religious or secular – are constructed from imposed prescriptions and proscriptions that have nothing to do with Adult facts. God is what is left after the universe has been explained in the (Adult) science of any age.

Observably, in the secular cultures with which we are familiar, moral relativism and self-interest are increasingly more unbridled than 'enlightened'; residual moral absoluteness is still riding on the back of not-so-long defunct religiosity that, I believe, is unlikely to survive more than another generation or two of secularism.

At the other extreme, contemporary religious fundamentalism is a desperate, doomed-to-fail retreat into the longing for certainty. Fundamentalism is the bid to make God a fact, like scientific knowledge. Its literalism misses the point that there cannot be just one true interpretation of anything. Kant demonstrated the inescapably solipsistic nature of our ideas, the impossibility of objectively matching our ideas to reality. The mystery of meaning is inviolate; there is no literal truth; subjectivity rules the universe.

Out of its adherents' desperate terror of death, fundamentalism avows the absolute one and only unquestionable truth through privileged knowledge of God. Unavoidably, it must righteously murder all infidels, whose mere existence threatens its precariously teetering security. It is the goodness of Be Perfect escalated to insanity and evil.

Notwithstanding the perils of fundamentalism, there is also peril in nihilism. Absoluteness unites them. We need religion (or curious agnosticism) for the homage it pays to the magical thinking in all of us, which is based on our deep appreciation of the connectedness of the macro- and the micro-worlds. Negatively, it is superstition, which fears the badness of the universe; positively, it is prayer, which is not as is commonly supposed an appeal to God to make everything better, but the way in which we avow our agreement with God that everything is as it must and should be. We pray for rain in the rainy season, for harvests in the summer.

Moderately expressed, with awareness that we can never successfully compete with God for perfection, the religious attitude to life is the kindest, most tolerant, most upright way of life. Excessively expressed, it disintegrates into the most intolerant, evil, obsessive-compulsive, insane character disorder. So how can we resurrect God effectively?

Our idea of God, to be convincing to contemporary mankind needs to reconcile and synthesize the holism of the ancient world with the atomism of achieved scientific knowledge. My own prediction is that within this century there will be an ecumenical unification of all the monotheistic religions under the umbrella of astrology. Through astrology, I believe, we will be enabled to perform the necessary task of de-anthropomorphising God while still retaining his super-human awful power, loving protection, and unknowable will.

Our present collective crisis of consciousness represents the failure of the false notion of materialistic science as the face of God. We cannot manage without God because our deepest need to believe in a 'meaning' and 'purpose' beyond our capacity fully to comprehend is timeless and universal in the face of pain and death. The religious orientation sees the interconnectedness of all things and events, sees each human being as a particular manifestation of God, sees everything being the way it has to be, and sees the beauty of each moment in its unique blending of hourly, monthly, yearly, and epochal cycles.

Astrologers are deeply religious people, steeped in awesome wonder at the order and meaning in the universe and the appreciation of even the smallest details of our lives as manifestations of the working of the Whole. 'Planetary influence' is not an alternative to a monotheistic view but a reinforcement of it.

The sixteenth century theologian Ronsard wrote:
"When evening casts its shadow o'er my eyes,
Musing on what's to come, I scan the skies.
Where God has written, clear for all to see,
The chequer'd course of human destiny.
For sometimes, leaning from His high abode,
By pity moved, He points us out our road,
Foretelling in the stars, His runic signs,
How good or ill this way or that inclines;
But men, by cares and fear of dying vex'd,
With eyes turned earthwards, scorn to read His text."

Astrology is God-minus-his-long-white-beard, who told us in the first chapter of Genesis that He has made available to us clues to His will through 'lights for signs and seasons, for days and years.'

Mundanely, our free-will is contained in the responses we make to our fate. Our responses are our choices and we cannot avoid choosing. Passivity is the self-delusion of no-choice, but of course it is a choice and, like all others, has consequences. Every choice we make is the cause of the inexorable train of events that follows in its wake, to the natural conclusion of a happening in our lives. When a happening is painful we are loath to remember the moment of choice that determined it, although often our admission of responsibility is implicit in our obsessive fear of the concluding pain – too late – and a conscious struggle to avoid it. In our most intense moments we do know (in our hearts) the simple truth that in virtually – if not absolutely – everything that befalls us we get exactly what we set out to get, and so what we deserve.

Much of our 'fate' is equitable with the potential and the limits of our genetic inheritance, which grants us three broad options of free-willed response. They are: *resentful envy* (being five feet tall and wanting only to be an Olympic high jumper); *passive, unambitious acceptance* (having a beautiful voice, but never getting any training, singing only for one's own pleasure); and *creative struggle*, in which we stretch the boundaries of our being to fulfil the nearly but not quite impossible in our natures, which option gives us the greatest possible satisfaction.

'Religion' is derived from the Latin word 'ligare', meaning to connect. 'Religare' means to reconnect ourselves to what underlies existence. What is man? What is the universe? How are the two related? Spirituality is our consciousness of these questions and desire to ponder them. Religions are our maps of the territory.

We are inside the universe as a given part of it and, by definition, the part cannot understand the whole. The goodness of religion consists of our submission to this truth.

For the vast majority of the world's illiterate or semi-literate masses religion is the only distraction from their daily imperative of finding enough to eat. Religion keeps them righteous, despite their misery, for fear of God's retribution, and compensates their misery with the hope of reward, at least in the world to come. It is the concrete, dependency relationship (Adapted Child) to its autocratic parent. Only very few people on earth have enough time off from attending to their survival needs to indulge themselves in arguing about and with God, questioning his authority and even his existence (from which privileged position, of course, I have written this essay).

Be Perfect is the ultimately trusting, religious view of life. Hurry Up is the ultimately paranoiac futile view of life. Be Perfect keeps life ordered and safe, but we need some Hurry Up to release us from the fearful, rigid, stultification that Be Perfect can induce, and allow ourselves some daring and exciting adventures. There is no love without hate, no good without evil. We are hard-wired for duality, and all (Be Perfect) Apollonian religions wisely include some prescriptive rituals that allow for episodic (Hurry Up) Dionysian catharsis while maintaining the balance of power in Be Perfect's favour.

People who now regularly attend churches, synagogues and mosques are mostly middle-aged or old. And for most of them it is no longer to worship a fully believed-in God, but rather for the sentimental value of belonging and the security of familiar rituals. Most young Christians, Jews and Muslims do not resonate to these rituals, and generally attend places of worship with their elders only under sufferance. But what young people do resonate to – probably more than their elders – is the new yearning in the world for spiritual meaning in our lives, prompting many of them to defect to cults of one kind or another.

As for all doctrines, the sterility of religious orthodoxies has been a cyclically recurring phenomenon throughout history. Be Perfect and Hurry Up are in continuous dynamic tension in us, individually and collectively. All beliefs begin as Hurry Up heresies and end as ossified Be Perfect forms. Rejuvenation is achieved by a new heresy that reconnects us with the ideal that presently meaningless ritual once enshrined. Moderately expressed, all orthodoxies, in their conservatism, help us to feel safe while comfortably tolerating some dissent. Moderately expressed, all heresies, in their creativity, pay homage to the value of the orthodoxies that they are injecting with a flammable spark. It is when the harmonious dialectic between orthodoxy and heresy breaks down that their mutual appreciation is transmuted into an escalating battle for supremacy; the inherent goodness in each metamorphoses into evil; they collide in unitary insanity, where murder and suicide become indistinguishable.

Perhaps part of the solution may reside in us re-examining our presumptuous pride in monotheism as a positive evolutionary achievement in human consciousness.

At the height of the Israeli-Palestinian conflict, Jasper Griffin in *The Spectator* (April 2002), with emperor's-new-clothes simplicity, asked if monotheism is, in fact, a degradation of polytheism in its intolerance and righteous pugnacity. He said, "Monotheism's first commandment, 'Thou shalt have no other gods before me', is a statement of exclusivity and intolerance. Is there not something a lot more civilised in polytheistic religions that allow their own and others' gods (and people) respectfully to co-exist? There was ... something to be said for pagan days, when a new god could be signed up and expected to fit in with all the rest in a spirit rather like that in which a soccer club transfers a star player from another team."

Could it be that present-day fashionable 'inter-faith dialogue' is the precursor of our cyclical reversion to the existential satisfactions of polytheism?

Glossary of T.A. Terms

ADAPTED CHILD. That part of the CHILD EGO STATE that is learned, as contrasted with the FREE CHILD, which is innate. The Adapted Child is acquired mostly between the ages of about one and three, in the form of rigid rules restricting expression of the FREE CHILD. At this stage of development, such rigid restrictions are necessary for the socialisation and safety of the child because her ADULT is not yet sufficiently developed for her to be reasonable, and her PARENT, which will later express care and control of herself and others, does not yet exist.

ADULT. The EGO STATE that contains knowledge and skills. It first appears in the 'whole self' at about one year of age, and grows most rapidly from then until about three years of age, and again between the ages of about six and twelve, although it is capable of continued growth throughout life. Its function in the 'whole self' is to store, process and access information it receives from the environment, and to make sense of life by reconciling its own information with the values of the PARENT and the feelings of the CHILD.

ALTERNATIVES. The outcome of the effective collaboration of the ADULT and the CHILD.

CHILD. The EGO STATE that contains feelings and impulses. It is the only EGO STATE we are born with. At first, it is only capable of instinctive experience and expression of overall satisfaction or overall distress, but it develops, both naturally and by conditioning, the capacity to experience and express a wide range of differentiated feelings and impulses. Its most rapid development takes place in the first three years of life.

COMPROMISE. The outcome of the effective collaboration of the PARENT and the CHILD.

CONFUSION. The content of the CONTAMINATION of the PARENT and the CHILD.

CONTAMINATION. A maladaptive, pseudo-resolution of an IMPASSE between EGO STATES, in which the incompatible impulses or attitudes of the relevant EGO STATES are expressed in a single, inauthentic idea or attitude.

DELUSION. The content of the CONTAMINATION of the ADULT and the CHILD .

EGO STATE. One of the 'sub-selves' that go to make up the 'whole self' of every human being. These are the PARENT, the ADULT, and the CHILD.

FREE CHILD. That part of the CHILD that is innate (as contrasted with the ADAPTED CHILD, which is conditioned). It contains, and expresses spontaneously, feelings and impulses that are authentic and appropriate to its desires and reactions.

GAME. A set series of inauthentic, ulterior TRANSACTIONS, ending in habitual NEGATIVE STROKES for both parties. Games yield high-value STROKES with high vulnerability.

IMPASSE. The experience of an unresolved disagreement between two EGO STATES, when they are equally energised, and neither will give in or make concessions to the other.

INDECISIVENESS. The experience of an IMPASSE between the PARENT and the ADULT.

INTIMACY. A candid, FREE CHILD to FREE CHILD relationship, without ulterior motives, reservations, or exploitation, from which the most valued STROKES are obtained, but which is also associated with the greatest psychological vulnerability.

JUDGEMENT. The outcome of the effective collaboration of the PARENT and the ADULT.

PARENT. The EGO STATE that contains values and beliefs and moral principles and generalisations about life. It is basically formed between the ages of about three and six through explicit exhortations by our parents concerning caring for and controlling ourselves and others. In grown-up life, the Parent is capable of modification and growth, to the extent that we may reject old values and acquire new ones as a consequence of new experiences and meetings with new, admired people. But, by and large, our Parent remains committed to the principles it was taught in early childhood. Its function in the 'whole self' is to enable us automatically to behave in ways that are conducive to our own and others' wellbeing, including the monitoring of our FREE CHILD, by granting it indulgences or imposing constraints, in accordance with the Parent's principles. In its constraining of the FREE CHILD, the Parent often looks like the ADAPTED CHILD, but the Parent acts in accordance with general principles, and may be flexible, whereas the ADAPTED CHILD is utterly rule-bound and rigid.

PASTIMES. TRANSACTIONS that yield medium-value STROKES with medium vulnerability.

PERSECUTOR. One of the compulsive, maladaptive roles through which the ADAPTED CHILD expresses itself in a GAME. The Persecutor role is associated with an inauthentic feeling of righteous triumph.

PREJUDICE. The content of the CONTAMINATION of the PARENT and the ADULT.

RESCUER. One of the compulsive, maladaptive roles through which the ADAPTED CHILD expresses itself in a GAME. The Rescuer role is associated with an inauthentic feeling of being unappreciated.

RITUALS. TRANSACTIONS that yield low-value STROKES with low vulnerability.

STROKE. Any act of recognition given by one person to another. Our need for and quest for strokes is continuous and lifelong. When POSITIVE strokes – which make us feel good – are not available, we would rather get NEGATIVE strokes – which make us feel bad – than receive no strokes at all, that is, be ignored. At birth, we are only capable of appreciating the most fundamental strokes, that is, actual physical contact with another human being but, gradually, we learn to value as strokes a wide variety of symbolic substitutes for physical contact, from the slightly valued nod of a passing acquaintance to the profoundly grati-fying, 'I love you.' The strokes, both positive and negative, that we were often given us in childhood by our parents are the strokes we are most likely to seek and to get from other people, for the rest of our lives. These, our favourite strokes, are called our TARGET STROKES. We each have our own POSITIVE and NEGATIVE target strokes, respectively those that make us feel especially good, and those that make us feel especially bad about ourselves.

STRUGGLE. The experience of an IMPASSE between the ADULT and CHILD.

TRANSACTION. Any interaction between people, irrespective of whether or not words are spoken. All transactions involve the giving and getting of STROKES.

VICTIM. One of the compulsive, maladaptive roles through which the ADAPTED CHILD expresses itself in a GAME. The Victim role is associated with an inauthentic feeling of being unfairly deprived.

WITHDRAWAL. The choice people make when they cut themselves off from all TRANSACTIONS and so receive no STROKES but maintain invulnerability to others.

WORK. TRANSACTIONS that yield high-value STROKES with high vulnerability.

Bibliography

Berne, E. *Transactional Analysis in Psychotherapy*, Grove Press, 1961

Berne, E. *Games People Play*, Andre Deutsch, 1966

Berne, E. *What Do You Say After You Say Hello?* Grove Press, 1972

Freud, S. *Civilization and its Discontents*, The Hogarth Press, 1963

Gleick, J. *Chaos – Making a New Science*, Heinemann, 1988

Gray, J. *Straw Dogs*, Granta, 2002

Jung, C. *Synchronicity*, Routledge & Kegan Paul, 1955

Klein, M. 'The accuracy of relationship description as a test of astrology' in *Correlation*, Vol. 8, no.2, December 1988

Klein, M. *Pain & Joy in Intimate Relationships*, Marion Boyars, 1993

Levi, P. *Survival in Auschwitz – If This is a Man*, (Translated from the Italian by Stuart Woolf), The Orion Press, 1959

Morris, J. *Conundrum*, Faber 1974

Nietzsche, F. *The Gay Science*, Vintage Books, 1974

Pascal, B. In Auden, W. and Kronenberger, L. *The Faber Book of Aphorisms*, Faber, 1962

Seymour, P. *Astrology: The Evidence of Science*, Lennard Publishing, 1988

Sheldrake, R. *Seven Experiments That Could Change the World*, Fourth Estate, 1994

Skinner, B. *Science and Human Behaviour*, Macmillan, 1960

Sobell, D. *Longitude*, Harper Perennial, 2007

Spinoza, B. *On the Improvement of the Understanding, The Ethics, Correspondence* (translated from the Latin by R. H. M. Elwes), Dover, 1951

Spitz, R. *The First Year of Life: a psychoanalytic study of normal and deviant development of object relations*, International Universities Press, 1965

**PSYCHE
BOOKS**

The study of the mind: interactions, behaviours, functions.
Developing and learning our understanding of self. Psyche
Books cover all aspects of psychology and matters relating to
the head.